Driving Backwards

Driving Backwards

Jessica Lander

TIDEPOOL PRESS
Cambridge, Massachusetts

For information, address TidePool Press
6 Maple Avenue, Cambridge, Massachusetts 02139
www.tidepoolpress.com

Printed in the United States

Library of Congress Cataloging-in-Publication Data

Lander, Jessica, 1987-
    Driving Backwards
    p.cm.
    ISBN 0-9914523-1-6/978-0-9914523-1-6
    1. Lander, Jessica 2. Gilmanton—New Hampshire
    3. Farm Life—New England—United States 4. Small towns—
    History 5. Country Life—United States—Anecdotes
    I. Title.

2014937617

To David
For the stories he shared

And to my family
For the stories we create together

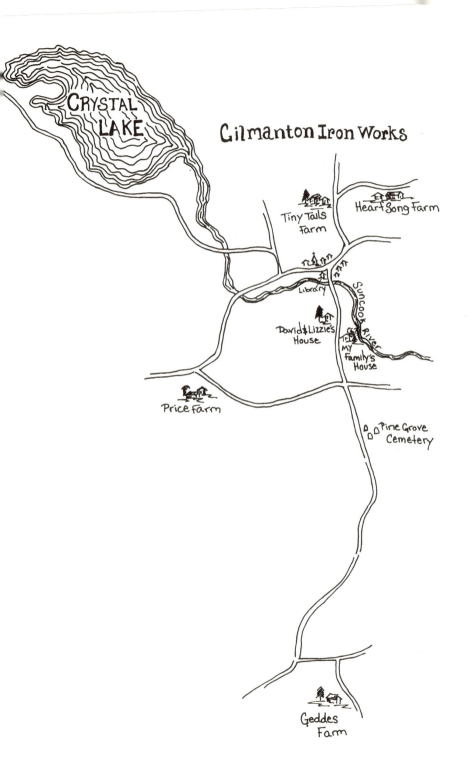

TABLE OF CONTENTS

Driving Backwards

IN TWO MONTHS, DAVID BICKFORD WILL TURN 100. One hundred is an age when memories have often faded with time, details become jumbled and lost, conversation turns repetitive. But, David has forgotten nothing. His memories are vivid pictures of the past. When he tells of neighborhood dances half a century ago, he remembers the day of the week and who was feeling under the weather. When a story includes a rainstorm, likely as not he knows the number of inches that fell. David recounts stories as if they happened the previous day. Nearly one hundred years of yesterdays.

Now, David lives alone. He buys his own groceries, mows his own lawn and grows his own robust tomato plants in plastic pots next to the house. David used to feast on tomatoes as a teen, eating them as you would an apple, but he has since developed allergies. Nevertheless, each year finds him checking fastidiously for hornworms and laying fertilizer.

Four years ago in 2009, David's roof developed a leak. He

climbed slowly, methodically, up to patch it himself. He gathered sheets of asphalt roofing and caulking for the journey. He took with him too a four-pronged cane that usually rests by the door. The cane is a precaution only, an occasional means of steadying against the slant. In public, he never employs the cane. "It would," he confides, "make me look like an old geezer!"

Wrinkles collect like a maple bark along David's neck, but hardly any place else. His voice is low and soft around the edges. He laughs often. When he smiles, wrinkles do appear: his whole face crinkles upward. His hands are burled; his fingers angle out. His handwriting is tight and precise. He favors red ballpoint pens. David dresses simply, in white button-downs tucked into slacks— blue or olive-green. He bends to tie his own shoes and, when he rises again, he mimics pines in verticality. David credits his elongated countenance to Native American ancestry, four generations back. He wears thin-rimmed oval bifocals over light blue eyes and each day he reads two local newspapers in their entirety. He wears his white hair short. His next haircut will be free—a hundredth-year birthday present promised by his barber.

In nearly a century of living, David has been, among other things, a farmer, a carpenter, a mechanic, a fireman and a town selectman. I know him best as a storyteller.

—៱៱—

David has lived almost his entire life in a single town in central New Hampshire. He has lived on the same road, in the same town, in the same village: Gilmanton Iron Works. He knows more about the town than any other living person. This is no small thing: Gilmanton was once the most famous town in America.

Visitors from across America once drove north and south and east and west through the windy roads of New Hampshire in search of Gilmanton. They came with well-thumbed copies of the same racy blockbuster and they accosted town residents in search of stories.

Gilmanton is neither the smallest town, nor the largest town in New Hampshire. It is not the oldest, nor is it the youngest. At sixty square miles, Gilmanton commands a domain equal to that of the entire Germanic country of Liechtenstein. It is double the area of Manhattan, although with approximately 3,700 residents, the town supports a populace roughly one five-hundredth the size. No grand bodies of water or grizzled cliff faces can be found within the town boundaries, although rivers, lakes, ponds and ragged knolls do exist. Gilmanton is fashioned almost entirely of hills and valleys—a great egg-carton landscape.

Shaped like a house—peaked roof included—the town of Gilmanton is most lively at the edges. The population congeals at two locations, Gilmanton Four Corners and Gilmanton Iron Works. They are the antipodes of the town, and like terrestrial poles, the two centers are opposing: the former is thick with white cape houses, the historic well-to-do; the latter a mottled collection of dwellings old and modern, the factory end of town. Enmities were tilled into the soil so deeply that when David was a kid, teens of the two villages were forbidden to date one another. For some time Gilmanton's two villages supported separate general stores, libraries, town halls, police stations, and a fire station apiece. Noah would have felt at home.

Half a century ago, Gilmanton's stories were read across America. But not anymore. Gilmanton has slipped from America's memory, just another small town now. But, David has forgotten nothing.

—ɯɯ—

Ninety-eight years ago the center of Gilmanton Iron Works— short of a mile from David's childhood home—went up in flames. The fire grew in the small hours of the morning and by midaft-ernoon engulfed much of the town's economic center. Twenty shops and river factories burned to the ground. It was the third economic catastrophe to strike the town, and Gilmanton would never fully recover. The first began just after the Civil War. When local youth who fought in Chancellorsville and Gettysburg discovered that the nation contained more hospi-table farmland than the Granite State's rocky fields, they packed their bags and migrated south and west. The second came twen-ty years later when railroad lines were laid and circumvented Gilmanton. By 1880, when David Bickford's father arrived by carriage in Gilmanton at the age of nine, everyone else in the town seemed to be leaving to more prosperous parts: to farms in the Deep South, to wide expanses in the Far West.

Among this exodus was one Herman Webster Mudgett, who left town just as Bickford was arriving. As David's father was setting up as a farmer and carpenter in Gilmanton, Mudgett ad-opted the alias H. H. Holmes and took up residence in Chicago as a well-to-do doctor. During the course of the 1893 Chicago

World's Fair, Holmes would become America's first serial killer. He never returned to Gilmanton, being executed out of state seventeen years before David was born.

Eighty-six years ago a teenage David trained a woodchuck to waddle at his heel. "We called him Chucky and he lived under the woodworking shop. I would call him out for lunch and he would come out blinking his eyes and lie on my lap. I used to tickle his belly and he would take hold of my finger, but he wouldn't bite it. If I was working in the garden he would be right out with me. One time I fed him some peas from the garden and the next day I happened to look outside and see he was out there eating the peas. 'Gee, now we're in trouble if my father finds out.' But I think my father took a liking to him."

Eighty years ago David drove his very first car, a Model T Ford, down the unpaved roads of Gilmanton. He can still direct me to the cottage of Harold Michael—up Crystal Lake Road at the upper end of the lake across the little bridge, first cottage on the right—who was the first owner of the car. "But I didn't buy it from him," David adds, always fastidious. David bought the car, engine shot, for $25 from a man named Warren Eastman who bought it from Harold Michael for an unrecorded sum. Eastman, David adds, lived on White Oak Road, just a turn or two past his house. David needed a crank to start the car in the winter and a stick to measure the gas. The engine was gravity-fed from the gas tank. When the gas got too shallow, the only way to climb a hill was to turn the car around and crest the summit in reverse. David recalls driving backwards over the hills of Gilmanton on numerous occasions.

David can recall in detail every time he got stuck in the mud, a regular spring phenomenon in rural New Hampshire. There was one trip to a brother's house that became an hour of shoveling and wedging rocks, taken from a nearby wall, under the tires. On another occasion during mud season, he drove his Model T to go court a young woman, Lizzie Twombly, whom he had met apple picking. On the rise to her house David's car got stuck good. "I had to get a neighbor who brought his horse with him to help pull the car out." On Stage Road boys made three dollars for every car they helped extract from the mud all the way up to 1956.

Eighty years ago David successfully courted Lizzie, mud notwithstanding, and married her at the Gilmanton parsonage. "When we married we were in the midst of raising a dairy barn—120 by 40 feet—for John Osman, with wood salvaged from the Hussey Factory: six days a week at two dollars a day. Liz's brother got married on a Thursday evening, we got married the Sunday after and another fellow working on the job married a school teacher right around then." Before they married, and when not driving, David used to jog the three miles to Lizzie's house to court her. After they married they moved down the road to a small cape they would share for almost seventy years.

Sixty-five years ago David worked as a mechanic during the day, and at nights attended dances in Gilmanton. "We used to hold dances in the winter. Liz and I used to go together. Helen played the piano, John Webster used to play the violin, but he'd call it the fiddle. The ladies would bring supper. There were maybe a dozen of us. Helen had a particularly big house with quite a large room with no carpet and we would have little dances there. We would dance the fox trot, the waltz and sometimes the square dance. Well, others would dance, I would just clomp around." David pauses in the telling, looking out into a different room in a different decade. "Sometimes we would hold dances at the big Academy building in Gilmanton Four Corners. I remember we went to a dance once and I was thinking to myself that that girl Helen looked a bit flushed. A few days later I found out why. She got the mumps, and I got the mumps a week later."

Fifty-seven years ago a young housewife and recent arrival to Gilmanton collected stories she had heard around town. She shuffled the stories with living-room gossip and her own imagination. The result was a book that transformed Gilmanton into the most famous town in America. The country knew the town not by its given name, but by its nom de plume: Peyton Place. Fifty years ago, my grandparents talked about it. As my parents grew up, the name was iconic. The blockbuster novel was discussed in secret on college campuses and it was decried publicly in town centers. Curious readers came to Gilmanton, seeking to discern which stories were based in memory and which were nothing more than convincing fiction. Many more stayed away but regarded Gilmanton as an epitome of small town America.

Eighteen years ago, I met David.

David and Lizzie were the first to greet us when we moved into the two-century-old house at 810 Stage Road in Gilmanton. I was eight at the time and remember most the blueberry pie that Lizzie baked for my younger brothers and me.

From our front door, the Bickford's house stands just a hundred yards to the right, past a leaning white pine, a hairy quince, a slope of lupines and a fish pond that, forty years earlier, David had set with fieldstones for previous inhabitants of our house. David's house is small, a white cape similar to many others in town, with forest-green shutters.

As kids, we sought David out for stories. We listened to David tell tales of the crow that rode on his shoulder as a boy, of the arsonist he tracked as a fireman, of the bridge he repaired after a powerful deluge. In the Bickford's living room we shared seats on a floral print couch with Lizzie. Of the two pink armchairs, David always sat on the right. Above the TV, a buck's head, antlers still in adolescence, was mounted to the wall. Beside the armchair sat a police scanner. It had been many years since he was a town selectman, even longer since he was on the town's fire department roster, but David kept the police scanner all the same, forever tuned to the local frequency. Always listening.

Ten years ago Lizzie began to lose her memory. David knew she had Alzheimer's. For us the loss was subtle; she spoke less and listened more. David did not like to draw attention to her forgetfulness. With increasing frequency, she asked us how we were doing, several times in a conversation. She continued to dress in blue slacks and blouses colorful with blooming flowers; she often wore knitted cardigans. She sat on the couch, remembering less and less. As her mind began to wilt, David spoke more, told more stories, shared more memories—as if attempting to refill his wife's leaking memory.

Eight years ago at the age of ninety-five—at the time the oldest resident in the town of Gilmanton—Lizzie Bickford passed away. David laid her to rest on Stage Road. She had grown up at one end of the road and lived her married life at the other end. She was buried in between, in a cemetery across from the church less than a mile from our house. The funeral was small, the afternoon warm. Afterwards David sold their home in the Iron Works and moved north thirty minutes to live near his daughter.

—⁓—

David lives alone. He mows his lawn. He buys his own groceries, driving to the supermarket in a Ford Focus—his Model T Ford long gone. He reads the local newspapers and closely follows the Boston Red Sox, recording the results of each inning in tight precise red pen. David lives alone, but surrounded by memories. His wood-paneled living room, like a black-box stage, transforms into the setting for a century of recollections: hundreds of one-act plays—alive with characters, settings, and dialogue. Leaning back in the worn pink armchair in his living room, David invites me into his memories.

When David was younger than me, he and his brothers used to swim along the Suncook River, in river kinks that gouged deep into the banks, a turn or two below our house. On the sandy bank of Upper Suncook Lake, they beached their rowboat—sixteen feet—and from there they paddled up to the river's mouth and fished for trout, bass, foot-long minnows, and, once, a mud turtle. In the winter, David strapped skates to his feet and glided out on the lake to pull pickerel up through the ice. In the summer, he fashioned fishing poles from stripped saplings and twine. With his father and brothers, David stuffed shot bags with suckers and lugged them to an old portly gentleman by the name of Charlie Gilman, who kept them in crocks, fashioning *mille-feuille* of suckers and salt. They caught the suckers in the Suncook, where the fish convened en masse in the shade under bridges. With fish so thick that the water appeared scaly, David's father had only to lie flat on the bridge and spear them like shish kebabs. When the river below the bridge no longer thrashed, David would climb down stream and chuck rocks into the Suncook to drive the stragglers up. At night, asleep, these scenes play on loop in David's dreams. "You know," he remarks wistfully. "A lot of those things going on years and years ago, they're as fresh as if they just happened."

What does it mean to hold so many memories? To close your eyes and see play across your inner-lids a lifetime of images. I imagine it could be overwhelming, it could be easy to get lost in a slideshow of the past. I cannot possibly know—I have lived only a quarter of David's span. David, however, appears relaxed in the duality of his living.

It was not until I was a young woman that I began to listen more closely. As a kid I was more interested in doing than listening. Gilmanton was about bike rides to the general store for hot dogs and locally brewed maple-syrup soda. It was about churning the waters of Crystal Lake as I attempted the crawl and the backstroke; face-painting flags on the Fourth of July and selling homemade soap at Old Home Day. It was for afternoons unsuccessfully tracking deer, and successfully serving as crossing guard to crotchety snapping turtles with pebbled eyes.

But as I grew older I sought out David more frequently.

David's stories drew me in, but it was his preternatural memory that kept me. I found myself staying longer in the wood-paneled living room listening to the humble recounting of a hundred years of life in small-town America.

In that time David witnessed Gilmanton's population at its nadir and at its zenith. When David was a teen, Gilmanton had dwindled to a frail six hundred-plus residents, so sparse that if everyone stood equidistant from each other, one would have to walk the length of six Manhattan blocks to find another person. And David experienced the regrowth of the town, as new farmers, new doctors, new mechanics, new families moved in—an influx that let Gilmanton finally re-attain its population peak set just after the Civil War and then surpass it. With these new residents come new stories to record, new memories to be remembered.

—∞—

A chronicler of the town of Gilmanton might be tempted to dwell on the lives of the town's two most notorious residents. America's greatest serial killer of the nineteenth century and its most scandalous novelist of the twentieth century. One man. One woman.

But it has been over fifty years since Gilmanton was notorious. The pine forests have grown up once more around the town, engulfing once-expansive farmlands. Now, the forests are being cut down again, a man-made succession: prefab single stories and subdivisions overtaking pines along the periphery. Gilmanton is just a small town in America, no longer *the* small town of America.

And while the stories of Gilmanton's two most notorious residents remain alluring, these are not the stories I am interested in. David's nearly one-hundred years of memories have spurred me to seek out the quieter stories.

And so I have placed my pens and pencils and notebooks in a side-bag and wandered out into Gilmanton. I have hiked high into blueberry fields to speak with farmers and down into barns to feel for teal-tinted chicken eggs. I have spent afternoons tracing the meanderings of stone walls in search of two-century-old boundary markers, and I have burrowed into the basement museum to study sepia maps with crumbling newspaper accounts. I failed to locate Native American tribal grounds, but I discovered the origins of the village's curious name, the Iron Works.

These are the quieter, everyday stories of the men and women of Gilmanton. They are ordinary people living in just one of two hundred and twenty-one towns in the state of New Hampshire. But if one pauses to listen, it becomes plain that these ordinary characters are anything but.

With almost a hundred years of stories, David Bickford holds the twentieth century in his mind. From David, I learned to listen and to remember. And now it is my turn. I have set out to start collecting new stories, new memories. To begin preserving another hundred years of life in a small American town.

June

The road to Gilmanton Iron Works is full of turns. We drive back roads shaded over in maple canopies, skirt by ponds with the remnants of beaver dams and pass sagging barns that appear on the verge of collapse. As we drive closer, the gas stations and the doughnut shops and the small motels drop away. Houses retreat from the road. We drive by a collection of spotted cows and our dogs rush to the car window and snuffle wetly at the heifers as we pass.

Three miles to the house we take a right off Province Road and turn on to Stage Road, named for the stagecoaches that used to drive along its length. At the turnoff stands a whitewashed, antiquated, signpost. Nailed to the flats are white wood arrows with thick black writing: Belmont to the left, Alton and the Iron Works to our right, Pittsfield back the way we came. Follow the arrow to the Iron Works.

We drive to Gilmanton, New Hampshire, in June, after the school year has ended and the summer heat has turned the Boston air viscous. When we were little we used to devote a full morning to packing the van: T-shirts, shorts, bathing suits, chapter books, sketch books, stuffed animals. We drove north two hours and did not drive south again till the first inhales of September.

Our house at 810 Stage Road is a two-story white cape, surrounded by bushy yews. It is an old New England homestead, renovated over the years. The former carriage barn is now a small guesthouse, the horse barn a flower garden. From the road you can see only the house and the crown of the forest beyond. What you miss is the long hill, sloping down to the Suncook River where we swim.

By the time we moved to Gilmanton, David Bickford had lived on Stage Road for nearly eighty years, acting as caretaker for our house for forty of those years. Our family purchased the house from an aging Barbara Spangler, who was given the home by her mother Janet Fellows, who in the 1950s had asked David to convert the carriage barn into a guesthouse and take the horse barn down to its stone foundation to make room for her peonies. David was called upon to construct crutches for crab apple trees and to see Mrs. Fellows' goldfish through the winter, moving them from an outdoor pond to a bathtub in the garage. Mrs. Fellows was the niece of Carrie Edgerly Leyland. Leyland, who was born in the homestead in the midst of the Civil War, was known to David as Granny Leyland, taught at the Potter School two miles away and churned butter from the milk David brought her. Carrie Leyland inherited the house from her father, Asa Edgerly, who inherited it from his father, David Edgerly, who was born in 1792, quite possibly in the same house, newly constructed by his own father, Ezekiel. In more than two hundred years, our family is only the second to have owned the homestead.

For me, June in Gilmanton is synonymous with planting. Our planting cycle, dictated by the school year, is later than most. We

dig trenches for tomatoes, mound hills for squash and experiment with constructing teepee trellises for sugar snap peas. In
recent years we have added curling Japanese eggplants and fiery
Thai chilies to our garden patterning. I wield a trowel, wear
shorts and a tank-top and slap at mosquitoes that leave splatters
of blood, dust and mud up and down my arms and legs. If it is
hot I take the hose and submit my head to the spray. If still hot, I
run barefoot down the hill and dive fully clothed into the gurgle
of the Suncook River.

June is a time of new beginnings. A week after planting, seed-
lings emerge shyly from the soil. Ideas germinate too.

A Tiny Two Acres

"Tiny Tails" reads a green and black lettered sign. Earlier it-
erations included: "Knuckle Dragger Farm" with the motto
"where cavemen still roam free," and "The Hermit & Blondie."
The "cavemen" alluded to a long-limbed neighbor; the hermit
and the blondie referred to the farmers themselves: Jim and
Cheryl Barnes. The Tiny Tails pays homage to thirteen horses
in residence, whose tails and indeed entire bodies appear to have
seriously shrunk in the wash. On two-acres in Gilmanton Iron
Works, Jim and Cheryl breed miniature horses.

Barrel-chested and slender-legged, Cheryl's horses are equal
in size and weight to a St. Bernard, although they slobber less.
To qualify as a Size A, a miniature horse must measure 34 inches
or less from hoof to withers, the point right behind the mane.
The babies stand a fluffy foot and a half at birth. Horses for
hobbits.

Miniature horses first trotted within the rambling menagerie
of Louis XIV, where tiny equines were displayed alongside tigers,

condors, rhinoceroses, and elephants at the palace of Versailles. Bred for upwards of three centuries, miniatures have occupied society's extremes—as novelties for European's nobility and as beasts of burden deep in the coal mines of Europe and North America. Today minis are kept as companions to their larger counterparts, a miniature investment instead of stabling another full-grown horse. Others are trained as guide horses for the blind; like seeing-eye dogs, they travel everywhere—subways, taxis, escalators, and airplanes. While unable to support a rider's weight, minis compete in a variety of competitions—jumps, barrel races, walk-trot routines. The difference: the owner traverses the course on foot rather than on horseback; when the horse jumps, the owner leaps beside it.

Equines under 14.2 hands, or 56 inches, should technically be called ponies. But despite their stature, miniatures are widely considered horses. Cheryl assures me that her miniatures have the gentler personality of a horse, rather than the obstinacy that ponies typically display. The miniature's conformation, its body proportion, resembles that of a horse as well. The American Miniature Horse Association prefers miniatures whose proportioning, in absence of a reference, fool a viewer into believing they are full-sized. Cheryl's stallion, Total Eclipse of the Heart (but around the barn referred to as Black), has a trailing mane and tail of shoe-shined ripples and an athlete's physique. In appearance, he resembles a full-blood Arabian—until you approach and realize his head barely brushes your hip.

When Jim and Cheryl bought five acres of land just outside the Iron Works village ten years ago, horses (no matter the size) were not on Jim's checklist; lawns were. Jim was emphatic. He was finished with condos. "I wanted a place with a lawn to mow and snow to shovel." Cheryl, though, had grown up on a Gilmanton farm. Cheryl started slipping horses into casual conversation. Jim recounts of Cheryl: "You know, my sisters have horses, I would like to have horses someday." A month later: "You know I've been thinking about those horses, maybe when you retire ..." A few weeks later, "retirement" became "maybe next year." Cheryl had discovered miniatures. "Then one day in August she comes home and tells me: 'I have two horses coming in thirty days and I need you to build me a structure for them.'"

The original stable Jim hastily erected at August's end was outgrown almost instantaneously. A large, two-story barn now holds ten stalls, eight mares, three babies, and two rambunctious stallions—one palomino and one solid black. The stallions are Spartacus and Black. Maggie, a silver dapple and white pinto mix, is one of Cheryl's originals—twenty-two years old, thick bellied, and, for a miniature, large. Her foal, Tonto, has outgrown her. Splashed white and brown at birth, Tonto's splotches are fading to black, making him appear wet around the ears and eyes. Tessa is pure silver dapple, not pinto, but soft gray with spots of white like tiny lights shown through gauze. Tessa is the barnyard bully. Susie, cow-splotched and trailing a spindly-legged filly, Patches, is Tessa's favorite prey. There is Ginger (a honeyed hue), Maizey (blue roan), Tizzy (red and white dun) whose full name is Tiny and Tempestuous, or TNT. Cara (stone gray) is followed by a fluffy son, grayed cocoa and resembling a Steiff stuffed animal. Star brings the total tail count to thirteen—a baker's dozen in horseflesh. Her coloring is primitive: grays, browns, whites with a dark stripe painting the ridge of her back—the color is called grulla. As Cheryl describes, "If you clip behind her front legs and her ears, she has stripes like a Zebra." As for Cheryl herself, she is blue-eyed with blond hair, and, like her horses, she is small in stature.

Of the five acres of property, two are thick with pine, white maple, and sugar maple. One acre accommodates the house and its sloping lawn. The farm itself, like the horses, is of Lilliputian dimensions. Today Jim is behind the house, at the apex of where the farm truly begins. The day's project: the blueberry fence. In two years, Jim's hope is to have blueberry bushes as dotted as a Seurat, with enough produce to sell at the farm stand they have set up by the roadside. Right now, though, the bushes are decidedly scrawny—not a berry in sight. Chickens are the culprits. Propped on the bucket of a compact Kubota tractor, bright orange, Jim frowns at white plastic piping. "That's why I am so anxious to get this done," an exasperated Jim informs me. "Stupid chickens won't leave me any berries. Go away—go lay some eggs!" Foster, a black and brown Australian Shepherd, sprawls in the shade unperturbed by poultry. Jim is five feet ten with a craggy face and a chiseled and chipped nose. White hair grows profusely thick around the edges; a red bandana conceals a balding crown. A tidy beard hugs a protruding chin sending fingers up to meet a tuft of mustache. He favors heavy brown work boots, socks pulled up, faded camo pants, and a beige shirt reading: "Life is better when you're well-adjusted."

The blueberry fence of white pipes resembles the ribcage of

some hulking beast. It is a "design-as-you-go-project" of hand-cut piping slotted like K'NEX construction toys, standing seven feet tall and draped in netting. Jim prefers this type of project to the prefab shed he assembled yesterday. He bought the shed, which is to hold one of Jim's two ATVs, knowing it would be a tight fit, but the larger version cost substantially more. Jim is not perturbed. "I'll punch out the back, or maybe take off the doors and extend it that way."

Muttering fence measurements, Jim goes searching for a tape measure—first up to the shed, then back down past the barn, then to the tractor: "Well, I just walked six miles to find the tape measure," he exaggerates. "But I think I remember putting it over here." He extracts the elusive tool from behind the tractor seat. After marking a length of pipe, Jim is off again in search of an extension cord, then a power saw, and a fourth trip for a special purple-tinted cleaner to paint the pipe ends. "I'm a terrible judge of how long something will take. If I really stuck with it I could probably do this in a day. But then I would have to find something else to do."

Everywhere he goes, so too does a blue three-ring notebook—a version of which he has kept for twenty-five years. He refers to it as "The Big Blue Book of Brains," an informal collection of lists, notes, ideas, and records for the "inveterate list maker." In the Big Blue Book is a pen sketch of the blueberry construction, resembling a connect-the-dots puzzle. Another page has a list of seeds and supplies: 150 strawberry plants, garden fencing, swan gourds, acorn squash, summer squash, tomatoes, zucchinis, straw, purple beans, wax beans, red potatoes, blue potatoes, peas, parsnips, pumpkins, potting soil. The previous page: a list of "wants and needs," next to each item a price, and for those that are crossed off, the date of purchase, the store and the amount paid. This list, with a few already crossed and dated, includes: a banjo case, brown shirt, black belt, raincoat, sixteen-foot trailer, twenty-four blueberry bushes, toothpaste, garden seeds, music stand, lime, peat, and a kilt.

Further along is the outline of a sermon. The title: "Freedom to be Free," scribbled beside it: "Duh!" Jim is laughing heartily as he slices through piping. "Didn't know I was a minister, did you?" As he describes it, the urge to join the church in his mid-thirties took him by surprise. Already working as a salesman at Eastern Propane & Oil, where he still works, Jim had no previous religious inclination; the calling, he says, just came to him. Jim was ordained as an American Baptist minister and was sent promptly to a dwindling church with orders to close it. Jim planned to stay six weeks; however, "a couple little old ladies and a few little old men—who are like little old ladies" proved determined to keep the church running. Jim remained for six weeks … and three years more. From there, he moved to a church in Brentwood—fifteen miles from his home in Northwood and forty miles south of his future home in Gilmanton. During the next seven years, he transformed the tiny Brentwood church into a congregation that consistently sustained hundred-member turnouts on Sundays and twenty-five participants for Wednesday night Bible study. At the end of seven years, though, Jim left the church. Recently he felt the urge to return. He gave his sermon on "Freedom to be Free" two weeks ago to a nearby congregation.

The ministry was what worried Cheryl the most when she first met Jim. Each of them was coming from a previous marriage, and each had grown kids. Cheryl practiced the Japanese healing art Reiki; like oil and water, religion and Reiki seldom emulsified. Jim's views of such matters were different, Cheryl says. "He sees Reiki as a holistic method of healing, which it is, and is generally very accepting."

Cheryl knew nothing of Reiki until 1988. A practicing nurse in Epsom, approximately twenty miles from Gilmanton, Cheryl felt something was lacking. "I knew there was more than taking care of the gallbladder in Room 209. Western medicine is great, but it sucks at chronic cases." Reiki was only one of a basketful of holistic healing methods Cheryl researched. She tried classes in polarity therapy, foot reflexivity, aromatherapy, and acupressure. Two years after signing up for lessons in Reiki, she was ordained a Reiki Master. Reiki settles into three planes. Aspiring acolytes learn first to heal themselves, and perhaps their pets. With time, they heal others, and, when they master the art, they no longer require physical contact with, or even proximity to, their patients. As a Reiki master, the third and final stage, one is allowed to teach others. "When you get to the third level, your whole life changes," Cheryl stares off into the distance, pausing. She tries again, "I can just stand in a room and there will be a person or a horse in need and I will literally feel the energy flowing out of my hands." Friends have nicknamed her Lucky. "But Jim doesn't believe in luck, we call it blessings instead."

Before Reiki, Cheryl traced palms. She read contour lines in skin and surveyed the terrains of her client's character at a dollar a minute. "I was a very strange child. I had a vivid imagination. I saw ghosts. I talked to animals and believed they talked back to me." She studied palms alongside physics and biology in high school. After graduation, she and a friend opened a New Age store in Concord. Cheryl taught classes in palms, crystal balls, and astrology; her friend read tarot cards. These days, Cheryl doesn't practice these arts. Some clients grew addicted to having their palm lines interpreted, becoming, as Cheryl saw it, slaves to their skin. Her own palms remain unread. She stopped teaching Reiki when her first husband died, but at night, sitting in a stall with one of her miniatures, she keeps up her former calling.

—◊—

Interspersed among the pages of seed inventories and sermon snippets in Jim's Big Blue Book are song lyrics. The songs are not familiar, most are fragments only, and all relate to New Hampshire: The New Hampshire Lottery, New Hampshire Primary, The Mount Washington, The Kancamagus Highway, General John Stark, The Day the Old Man Fell. Jim learned guitar on a Kay at fifteen. He has kept the Kay, propped beside a twelve-string Guild, a six-string Gibson, a Woods banjo, and a Johnson mandolin. Folk music has always been his favorite. He plays with friends at small venues—they call their group, Just Plain Folk. Somewhere in an as yet unreadable future is an all-New Hampshire album.

The Big Blue Book is filled with lines, rhymes, stanzas, and a few chords written on the side. "I remember it so well / that sunny day in the spring / the day the Old Man fell." The next page: "There's got to be a reason for (pause) mud season / but what it is I really can't say / all I know is / I'll be so glad to see the (pause) / Middle of May." Of the scandalous best-selling local author Grace Metalious, Jim has composed: "A sordid tale of fiction but she told it oh so well / all about a small town with secrets behind its face / she wrote a racy novel and called it Peyton Place." A list of thirty-three possible song titles follow: "Frost Heaves and Potholes", "Ice Fishing", "Cutting Cordwood", "The Maple Syrup Song."

—ᴍ—

The next afternoon finds Jim splitting cordwood. His wood splitter compresses logs against a vertical blade, smoothly slicing wood into halves, quarters—a woodman's Exacto. Bough limbs and stumps are heaped in the brush. Jim is cutting hardwood (maple), which sells for four dollars a bundle up at the stand he has set up by the road. Pine and other softwood sell for only two. The stand, a wood cart curtained in potted perennials, is weighted with squash, syrup, rhubarb soda brewed by Cheryl's relatives, pies, jams, peaches, cookies, cornbread and eggs. A week ago, visiting grandkids made muffins to acquire extra pocket change for a fair. "I get a kick out of selling things to people!" Jim sees the farm stand as an investment for retirement. Cheryl thinks it's humorous that Jim wants to trade in a job, barely requiring physical labor or long hours, for one that demands an excess of both. Laughing, Jim agrees. "My goal is to utilize every inch of this property." Originally, the stand sold only firewood. Jim had hired men to log a portion of the forest.

"They left a mess, so I decided to cut the remaining wood and put it out near the road…one day I'm watching TV during vacation and a man comes to the door 'Hey, is that wood for sale or what?' 'Oh yeah.' 'Well there's no sign.'" Jim built a sign.

Eggs are the hottest commodity at the stand; three dozen disappear daily. Each night, Jim goes scavenging for eggs. He is hoping to top the summer record of fifty. One day, he finds forty-eight. Another day forty-six. Forty-nine. "Just two more." No luck. Up in the barn loft heaving down hay bales that night, I hone in on four white ovals nestled under an eave. Jim bounds up the ladder, but it is a false alarm. He passes one over, "You can tell how old they are by how much they weigh; the yolk dries up." Except for its oblong shape, the egg's weight suggests a Ping-Pong ball rather than tomorrow's breakfast. Neither Jim nor Cheryl has an exact tally of the chicken community scratching, dust bathing, roosting, and riding horseback in the barn. The count is well over 100.

At two eggs every three days, chickens lay productively for three years—if they can successfully evade the wildlife. Foxes consume the entire bird when they catch them; they feasted on twenty-seven last year. Raccoons are picky; they desire only the head. Weasels sever the head and drink the blood. If a rat finds a way into the barn, it will gnaw, beaver-like, at the legs of sleeping fowl. During the day, if a chicken wanders off the farm in search of grubs in the lawn next door, they are under threat of becoming paintball targets. But if they survive the wildlife and the neighbors, the chickens are free to grow into old doddering hens. Cheryl refuses to kill them.

Cheryl and Jim collect chicken breeds like other people collect antique tea cups: red hens, white hens, black hens, mottled hens, brilliant red-combed hens, long-necked hens with no comb, spike-headed hens which appear prehistoric. What began as a single Bantam and her babies has feathered out into an uncountable number of varieties and crossbreeds: Rhode Island Reds, New Hampshire Reds, Red Stars, Silver-Laced Bantams, Gold-Laced Bantams—honey with black lattices, Buff Cochins—"the golden retrievers of the chicken world," White Cochins—buxom grand duchesses with voluminous feathered pantaloons. Araucanas lay blue-and-green eggs, Cuckoo Marans chocolate-tinted, Speckled Hamburgs white. Black Sex-Links make awful mothers. "They'd just as soon eat their eggs." Bantam Cochins are often bought as house pets. "They'll sit on your lap." In the past, they've had White-Crested Black Polishes, Buff Minorcas, and Buttercups. Now there are Silver-Spangled Hamburgs, Partridge Cochins, Barred Rocks, Bearded d'Anvers, Mottled Cochin Bantams—Cheryl's favorite is named Snowflake, and Black Australorps. The Short-Legged Japanese Black Tail has plumage sweeping up and over like a painted fan. He is the only full-grown rooster in the barn, and like the horses, he is of miniature measurements.

At Tiny Tails Farm, large breeds often fare poorly. Two Broad-Breasted Bronze turkeys once stalked the yard—strutting, puffing out feathers in intimidating war dances. They laid siege to everything that moved, Jim, Cheryl and the local farrier included. Gleefully, Cheryl screens a thirty-second slide show: baby turkeys, full-grown turkeys, decapitated turkeys, plucked turkeys—34- and 38-pound feasts dubbed Thanksgiving and Christmas. The turkeys survived barely a season. The sheep that once mowed the farm were a considerably larger investment, but fared little better. Jim's response to Cheryl's growing horse herd was to retaliate with sheep. "Being of Scottish extraction I decided to raise Scottish Blackface," Jim shakes his head sadly. "Scottish Blackface are really not sheep," he confides, "in the same way that professional wrestlers are not really people." Weighing more than 150 pounds, they dress in long curly horns. These are not the fluffy frolicking variety. In Europe, they are used as land clearers—they eat everything—but not Jim's. "They were as fussy creatures as I've ever seen, they preferred grass, hay or nothing." For "two long terrible, nasty years" they wreaked havoc. Findlay the ram amused himself by pounding incessantly at the confines of his stall. One day, Cheryl arrived at the barn to find Findlay protruding from the barn wall—a living trophy head. That stall is now twice-lined with wood, though the crack in the wall's exterior remains. The ewes, lambs and one rambunctious ram have gone to other homes.

Cheryl was raised with sheep. Her childhood brimmed too with cows, pigs, chickens, and, during one two-year period, twenty-two horses. In addition, Cheryl expanded her family to include rats, snakes, and miscellaneous roadside victims. She once adopted a hawk hit by a car, and a deformed chicken named Harriet. A baby woodchuck, who sustained a dislocated hip from the family poodle, dined for months on evaporated milk, corn syrup, and egg yolks. In fourth grade, a garden snake became her show-and-tell; Cheryl knew her teacher was terrified of all things slithering. In nursing school, a black-and-white hooded rat named Rachel attended classes in anatomy and pathology, commanding a view from Cheryl's shoulder or from the front pocket of her overalls.

Years later, Cheryl's nursing home office was partially converted to accommodate a baby snapping turtle, only four inches long. He denned under her desk for three years, feasting on Wal-Mart brand turtle food and taking sink baths with Cheryl as attendant, wielding a toothbrush for a loofa. When time came to release the turtle into the wild, Cheryl purchased, as a going away present, twelve goldfish—a lesson on live food dining. "He would sit stone cold and then a fish would swim by and you wouldn't even see his head come out, but the fish would be gone."

Cheryl is off to feed and water her charges. Jim stops her to inquire about a red dot the size of a quarter on the back of his thigh. Cheryl inspects. "That's Lyme disease," she informs him in a no-nonsense voice. "That's the tick you said wasn't infected and was. You need to be on antibiotics. You need to go to the doctor tomorrow." Jim is aghast—not at the Lyme disease but at the prospect of having to go to the doctor. "But I pulled the tick out, do I really have to?" Jim looks put out. "I'll put it simply," says Cheryl, her voice hardly sympathetic. "You could leave it and be in excruciating pain for the next three years, or you can take antibiotics and have it cleared up in a week. Are those plain enough terms?" Cheryl continues down to the barn. "How about a beer remedy?" Jim calls after her, grinning. Jim is only joking; he hasn't touched alcohol since 2006.

Cheryl attended Concord Hospital School of Nursing imme-diately out of high school. She enrolled in a three-year program that set her squarely in the middle of daily hospital activity. She and her peers worked in the state hospital nights and week-ends. In their third year, they took command of an entire floor. At twenty-six, she became the youngest director of nurses at Epsom Manor Nursing Home. After five years, she switched permanently to nursing the elderly. "They have lived their lives. They make sense, even when they are not all there." Often Cheryl ferries the farm to the grandfathers and grandmothers of her nursing home. She brings Bantam chickens that sit calmingly on patients' laps. She passes around rabbits: long-haired English Angoras with tufted ears, maned Lionheads and Jersey Woolies resembling hopping pompoms. On occasion even the miniatures will make an appearance in the Day Room.

Nursing is a twenty-four hour investment: humans by day, horses by night. Miniature horses, like humans, are among the rare examples of animals requiring assistance at birth, which is unusual as reproduction is essential to the survival of a species. Bred to be tiny, miniature babies are briefly considered enormous, being dangerously large both in the womb and during the birth. Human help is routinely required. Cheryl notes that roughly one in four unassisted births is fatal for the foal, the mare or both. With one hand on Tizzy's rump, Cheryl checks the expectant mother's udders. Close to foaling, there are specific signs she seeks. The udders expand with enriched milk; a hollow appears along the back and in front of the hind legs as the foal drops low in the belly. There are other more subtle signs. "They get what I call Jell-O butt: all the muscles relax." Cheryl presses fingers into Tizzy's butt—still firm. Relaxed muscles also produce what Cheryl terms "rag doll tail." Gently she takes Tizzy's tail and swishes it back and forth; there is still some resistance. Tizzy stands calmly through the whole examination, snuffling her bucket for overlooked grain pellets. Cheryl repeats the procedure with Star across the aisle. Neither mare is closer than a week away, Cheryl predicts. There are other, more subtle symptoms. Horses close to delivery might kick at their belly or rub their hind feet together like crickets. Agitated tail swishing can be another indication of imminent labor. It can also testify to large swarms of flies.

In past years, Cheryl's mares have gone vacationing at other barns for their birthing. This year they are staying home. Miniatures often foal between ten at night and four in the morning. Tonto, Sunny, and Patches poked heads out at 10:30 pm, 7:35 a.m., and 4:00 a.m., respectively. To spare Cheryl from having to set up bed and blanket in one of the stalls, she has invested in two devices. Halter alarms hang like pendants around the mares' necks, paging Cheryl if they doze horizontal in the shavings. Set into the stall corners are the black unblinking eyes of cameras. The cameras stream live videos to a web site called Mare Stare. Cheryl watches her horses from work. So too do horse lovers in Concord, Cambria, Calcutta and Cancun who monitor hundreds of expectant equines.

Yesterday Jim and Cheryl were awakened by a ringing phone at 2:30 a.m. The caller: a Californian woman. "I'm calling to tell you that one of the horses has knocked the hay rack down." Another woman called to complain that the cameras were switching too rapidly; she couldn't follow the action. "What action?" Jim asks. Two days ago Jim was logging wood and was late cleaning the barn; he found a reprimand waiting on his answering machine: "You know, the buckets are all over the place it doesn't look like anyone is home. Will you please call and let us know what is going on?" A few weeks ago someone called, positive a foal was stuck half in half out. Cheryl diligently investigated. There was no foal, only a chicken roosting behind a horse.

—⁓—

The peach orchard blooms between the barn and the house—branches slung low, bearing walnut-sized nuggets of fruit—green and inedible for a month more. There are eight standard trees and a clump of three newly planted dwarfs. Dangling from the branches of immature trees are filled water bottles. I inquire as to why Jim's youngest trees are fruiting Dasani and Evian. "I'm festooning!" Weighting the branches allows sunlight to tickle the tree's core.

Splaying boughs is not the problem for the mature specimen;

the unripe crop has enthusiastically taken up the challenge. Fruit hangs so heavily that it literally tears off limbs. Today Jim plays bonesetter. We are off in search of twine. In addition to the standard and dwarf varieties, there are three Saturn peach trees near the road. They produce doughnut-shaped fruit—flat and dipped in the middle. As well, there are Cortland and McIntosh apple trees, one cherry, and two plum trees of the Ozark and Red Heart varieties. We collect twine from the shed, the first home of the miniatures, and return to the orchard to operate on peach trees. From a ladder's added height, Jim hoists partially broken branches gently up and over the barn's roof, securing them with slings of string.

Next, preventive care is administered to other trees—a mix of thinning and propping. For the second tree we need boards, and for that we follow a mud-splattered path to the Settlement. The clearing in the woods boasts a steadily expanding collection of buildings: The Guard House, the maple syrup Sap House—one story with a steeply pitched and vented roof allows escape routes for sap steam. Instead of sap buckets, tubes run like strings of holiday lights from tree to tree to tree. The tubes sip sap from tree trunks, before expelling the liquid out into large white barrels. Jim reckons he taps 180 trees a season. In the Settlement too is the Schlepper House and a collapsed shed, still containing a mower, brush chipper, and the log splitter, referred to as SILTS: Settlement Implement Lean-to Structure. "I try to name everything," Jim explains.

We head back, two old wooden boards heavier—up the dirt road with Foster, the Australian Shepherd, and a lone chicken leading the procession, up past the garden and the shed and the far paddock and the lower paddock and Black's ceaseless pacing. Back in the orchard, wooden boards transform into makeshift crutches for peach boughs. On other trees, blue and yellow ladders perform the same task. Supporting another sagging branch is a red and white door, the middle an empty void where glass once was. In the vacant window is framed a tableau: a corner of the barn, a sugar maple, a peach limb, a ferreting chicken, and, whisking in and out of the frame, a golden tip of a tiny horse's tail.

At the Rocks

WALKING ALONG THE ROAD to the center of the Iron Works in early June I can barely make out the remains of Mill Road—overgrown and partially consumed by jewelweed, milkweed and poison ivy. Volunteers of curving maples act as camouflage. For years I walked past it and biked past it and never knew it was there. It was only when I learned that there was once a road lined with mills that I began to scrutinize the forest edge, which slopes up the bank to the library and village center.

Jogging along the river, the dirt road is paved in leaf litter, pine needles, and troughs of mud. To the right, the land rises steeply. Backsides of barns peer down haughtily. To the left, glossy green water slips by, relaxing from a frothy kneading farther up the river. Woven into the tangle of leaves and vines tasting the river's edge sprout rusting rounds of metal: a car door, buckets, barrel strips. Near where eddies rasp the water surface, my eyes search out the masonry, as if adjusting to the dark; foundations materialize. A ring of stone circles fifteen feet wide, possibly a cellar, a workroom floor, a granite hitching post leaning lazily. A wall, stacked and chiseled blocks, stretches forty feet. Where the river widens, evening light is tossed glittering on the roughened surface.

No mills remain in Gilmanton Iron Works. Abandoned or burned, they once sat thick along the river. The Suncook's waters churned the first gristmill in the village back in 1770, nine years after the first settlers—a bedraggled couple—arrived by snowshoe. Within ten years multiplying mills scooped water in endless Ferris wheels: gristmills, sawmills, bark mills, lumber mills—fashioning clapboards, shingles. A soap factory, a rake factory, a plow factory, a tannery, a shoe shop employing seventy-five people, blacksmiths, cider presses. Stone mementos remain, like headstones. Mottled metal, granite foundations, the sloping stone buttress of a bridge veiled in a mossy shroud, and the Suncook River itself remain.

The Suncook River embraces the Iron Works, caressing the southern edge of the village—a post office, a general store, library, fire station, church—before curling under the bridge and wrapping around two-century-old, white wooden homes. Under the bridge, the water grows gruff over bulbous stones, then calm by a gentler curve, then talkative again as it sweeps back toward Elm Street, which becomes Stage Road just outside the village.

When the river reaches our house, it is chuckling, rising up and down in white caps. At its lowest, water laps at my calves. After a week of rain my waist gets soaked. Under the water, at the upper edge of our property, are the remains of a wooden dam we discovered years ago—just three smoothed trunks partially

embedded, the remnants of a lumber mill and cider press. When the water is particularly high, bonneting all protruding boulders, we run rafts down dwarf rapids.

The river slows as it emerges from the pines below our house—a stretch of rippled obsidian. A fifty-year-old dam, three feet high, fashions a swimming hole out of the river. Countless hours have been passed holding diving contests off the dam. Other times we sit below, water leaping off shoulders and heads in cascading fountains. The water of the Suncook, thrown dizzy over the dam, sounds thunderous when heard from below. Elsewhere the sound softens to a static hum.

Down past the dam the river courses. Down past the apple orchard, and kinks in the river bed—shallow, sandy bottomed. A jagged turn gouges a deep swimming hole. A strong current sweeps past dragonflies: iridescent blues, violets, aquamarines. Down past one bridge, two bridges, expelled down into the Upper Suncook Lake and the Lower Suncook Lake, no longer in Gilmanton but in Barnstead. Swirling down through Barnstead, and into Pittsfield, Loudon, Chichester, Epsom, Pembroke, Allenstown, and Suncook Village rides the river. Down, down, down into the rush of the Merrimack River. Water from the Suncook whisks with waters from Lake Winnipesaukee, Contoocook River, Artichoke River, Turkey River, Sohegan River, Soucook River, Shawsheen River, Spicket River. Down they stream, out of New Hampshire, into Massachusetts, hooking northwards and then out into the Gulf of Maine and the Atlantic.

The Suncook River runs 35 miles through central New Hampshire, bearing over 2,000 acres of water in all. It is not an especially large river, but neither is it insignificant. Thirty-five dams cause hiccups along the way. There are only two major dams, the Pittsfield Mill dam and the Northwood Lake dam in Epsom. Until recently there was another Epsom dam, the Huckins Mill dam, a hundred and forty years old and attached to what once was a riverside restaurant. On Mother's Day, 2006, heavy rain induced the Suncook to stretch its legs, stand up and move, settling down again in a sand pit and cornfields less than a mile away. The river cut straight southwest, leaving behind a rumpled, meandering bed two and a half miles long. The Huckins Mill dam is now silent; the riverside restaurant no longer affords a water view. The two thousand dollar bridge purchased by the restaurant owner to cross to Bear Island, once embraced by the river, is superfluous. Over a thousand endangered brook floater mussels were tagged and relocated to the new river bed. The Suncook's unpredicted jaunt was the largest in New Hampshire recorded history.

Like many New Hampshire rivers, the Suncook's name is Indian derived. The name is the only remaining tribute to an Abenaki Indian village where the village of Gilmanton Iron Works now stands. The exact location of the village is unknown. Some suggest it was along Crystal Lake. One man believes it sat up on the hill across the river from what is today Mill Road. Most Gilmanton residents are not aware there ever was a village, let alone that the Suncook flows as testament. The village was called Senikok, which in Abenaki translates to "at the rocks."

Two miles north of Gilmanton, nestled among Suncook Mountain, Heator Mountain, and Mt. Klem, Round Pond sits glassy surfaced. Round Pound is spring-fed, and it in turn feeds the Suncook Brook, which slips into Manning Lake, Sunset Lake, Crystal Lake, and from there into the Suncook River. Many point to Round Pound as the Suncook's headwaters, but the claim is contested. On the pond the wooden igloos of two beaver homes protrude out of murky water. Leeches, like black ribbons, three inches long, perform pole dances around reed stems. Farther down, the river glitters with fish. Over the course of the summer, the Suncook is stocked with trout: brow trout, brook trout,

rainbow trout. Last year more than 500 brook trout were re-
leased in Gilmanton. New Hampshire's smallest fish, the swamp
darter, two inches and blotchy, resides in healthy numbers. Lone
bridal shiners have been spotted. More numerous are: common
sunfish, ballfish, chain pickerel, longnose dace, largemouth bass,
smallmouth bass, white perch, horned pout, margined madtom,
white sucker, yellow perch, bluegill, golden shiner, redbreasted
sunfish.

Those who don't believe the true headwaters of the Suncook
flow out of the secluded Round Pond, point farther south to
Sunset Lake. Still others believe the river begins in the town of
Gilmanton, two miles above the center of Gilmanton Iron Works
at Crystal Lake. The lake's shore is set with summer homes, many
frequented by the same families for the last hundred years—
generations of swimmers. Residents fashioned hotels along the
shoreline: Hillsdale Farm; Highland Farm House; The Pines,
skirted round with an open-air veranda; The Whip-Poor-Will;
The Colonial; The Triangle; Glen Echo, served soft drinks and
fresh fish and came complete with a hewed-board bowling alley.
Families came by train, lugging trunks from New York City and
Boston. During summers at Crystal Lake, they rode horses to the
Iron Works to watch silent films and hopped fences to tempt cows
with chocolate bars. They hiked and fished and, from rocking
chairs, shot ducks off the lake's glassy veneer. They dove into the
chill of Crystal Lake in body-tight wool knit. Others swam nude.

Years ago I learned to swim in the shallows of Crystal Lake.
Now I swim out far, turning onto my back to float. I take a canoe
and paddle with my brothers out to the sandbar. Sometimes I

kayak. Once I came across a family of feeding loons. I drifted for a time watching the parents dive again and again for fingerling fish.

Crystal Lake was once known as Lougee Pond, just as Gilmanton Iron Works was once called Avery Town. John Lougee of Exeter purchased land on the western edge of the lake in 1778, and the name remained active for a hundred years. In the same year that Lougee arrived in Gilmanton, Moses Morrill decided to try his hand at an unusual form of mining.

Bog iron collects in swamps, bogs, ponds or lakes, where water is heavily seasoned with soluble ferrous hydroxide. Exposed to high levels of oxygen and alkaline, ferrous hydroxide undergoes a chemical transformation, precipitating out into impure iron deposits of ferric hydroxide. The iron in Crystal Lake rests twenty feet below the surface. To obtain the metal, Morrill fashioned elongated tongs, clasping the iron like chopsticks pinching rice grains in the depths of a soup bowl. The iron was sent a mile down the Suncook to a smelting factory along Mill Road. Melted, hammered, plied, the lake's iron was fashioned into horseshoes, Shaker style stoves, cooking utensils, door hinges, plows, latches, anchors. One story suggests that Crystal Lake iron is immortalized in an anchor of the U.S.S. Constitution. No records confirm the legend.

The Iron Works along the Suncook spawned mills up and down Mill Road in the center of a town once called Avery. But the mining of Crystal Lake was not a decade old before the project and the oversized tongs were abandoned. The iron was too scarce and the means of extraction too onerous. However, other mills continued to spin river water up and over, up and over for a century more. In time though, they too would close, burn, decay. But the name adopted by the village along the Suncook River, when bog iron was once extracted from a lake, would remain. Gilmanton Iron Works.

Raising Kids

VALERIE JARVIS HAD a predicament. Nowhere could she find farm clothes for women. Farm pants, work boots, sturdy gloves. All were measured, cut and sewn to men's proportions. "Women in farming are still something of an anomaly," Valerie explains. When she calls up farm service agencies they can't quite believe she runs her own farm. Valerie wears her strawberry blond hair short. In her late forties, she is lithe and commanding. She drives a gold Volkswagen bug. She has sharp blue eyes and favors silver hoops in her ears and a silver stud in her nose. At farm stands she wears loose flowing cottons and linens. In the milking room, surrounded by goats, she wears no-nonsense farm clothes—Men's Small.

Valerie did not always intend to raise goats. When she and her family first moved to Gilmanton from Pennsylvania in 1994 they limited themselves to a dozen chickens. Next came a horse called Cookie, as Valerie was fond of riding. But Cookie needed a companion and rather than buy another horse, the family picked out a black and white Nigerian Dwarf goat—Snickers. Snickers, too, was lonely. Along came dairy goats. Within twelve years, Valerie's primary focus was raising kids. On Heart Song Farm, as she christened it, Valerie was mother to sixty-five goats and ten home-schooled children.

We stand in the milking room—humans to the right, goats to the left. Four goats at a time come through a small door and onto the milking ledge where they are hooked up to the machines. Each goat takes three minutes to milk. Valerie currently has fifty lactating nannies on the farm. Milking takes place at 7:30, morning and evening. The total daily yield supplies Valerie with forty gallons of fresh raw goat milk for her to turn into cheese.

Years ago Valerie loved to milk all the goats by hand. "The rhythmic motion, the breath of the goats on your arm … it was sort of a tranquilizer for me … a get away from the hubbub of the house." That was when she had only eighteen goats to tend. However, milking the growing herd triggered carpal tunnel syndrome, and she had to hand the process over to machines.

Every baby goat raised on the farm is bottle-fed by Valerie and her own children. She used to allow the mothers to nurse for a couple of days, especially when there were twins, but the two kids would fight over the same teat resulting in lopsided udders—throwing off the goat milk production for the year.

Valerie keeps baby goats in a pen in the barn. Reared on the bottle, they clamber for attention whenever a person walks by—spindly legs and quarter-round hooves finding purchase on the wood walls so that their long necks stretch up to waist height. For the littlest, I present a finger, which they latch on to, thinking it a bottle or a teat. With no teeth yet, their persistent suckling is strangely ticklish.

—⁓—

Heart Song Farm is tucked away at the end of a meandering steep dirt path off a gravel-strewn Tibbetts Road. The road is lined with new growth forest on either side, but when you drive onto the farm the landscape opens up into long swaths of meadow and fields. The house and barn run in a long connected line, additions added upon pre-existing additions. There is a shed for a dozen bikes, a pond, and a tire swing. The daughter of a military man, Valerie spent her childhood roaming America, living in eleven places within twelve years. "I really wanted my kids to feel like they had roots, connections, respect for life. I wanted the kids to have a family. I wanted a place where my kids would want to come home to. I wanted them to have memories of working together." Valerie wanted a farm. When her husband Bill's IT job brought him to Alton, they searched for houses in towns nearby. Standing in a field looking over the hills of Gilmanton for the first time, Valerie felt her heart sing. The name stuck.

To the right of the sprawling house and barn, hidden by the tall grass is an airstrip. That was one of the original draws of the farm. When Valerie was a child, her father used to let her ride with him as he learned to fly in New Mexico. Twenty years later Valerie decided she wanted to learn to fly herself. In 1994, the year she purchased the farm, she received her pilot's license. "It was a challenge. I didn't think I could do it, but that's all it takes: if you tell me I'll never do it or if I tell myself that, then that's all I need to go ahead and do it." Pregnant with her sixth child, Valerie familiarized herself with the undulating hills and pine filled valleys of Gilmanton, from an altitude of ten thousand feet. Valerie no longer feels a compulsion to fly. But sometimes, while floating along the Suncook, I'll look up to see the colorful curve of a hang-glider and know one of Valerie's kids is up there.

When I was eight, I learned to swim strokes off the sandy beach at Crystal Lake. It was Valerie's two oldest—Matt and Mark—who taught me. As kids, we used to play together along the river. In addition to Matt and Mark, there was Hannah, Jesse, Tabitha, and baby Levi. And, soon there was Libby.

Around this time Valerie began experiencing abdominal pains. She found that the raw goat milk she collected soothed her stomach. Intrigued, she got a few more goats and began pouring tall glasses of goat milk for the entire family. "With all the small proteins that are easy for the body to absorb," she remarked, "goat milk is the closest thing there is to breast milk." Soon, goats begat goats begat goats. By the time Valerie's eighth child, Moriah, was born, the house was overflowing with goat milk. Out of curiosity and excess, Valerie turned to cheese making.

—m—

The milking is finished and the last of the goat quartets have exited right—back to the yard and their feed. We head to the adjacent cheese room, the milk preceding us through tubes and tanks. The cheese room, like the milking room, is compact. White walls, stainless steel counters. The ceiling is low, the air heavy with a sweet and slightly sour aroma. An industrial door along the center wall leads to the cool-room where finished cheese is stored. Kept at 34 degrees, it contains over a thousand dollars in cultured curd. On the wall hangs an entire arsenal of slotted, flat-bellied spoons and pot-bellied ladles—Valerie's cheese-making equipment, amassed over three years. Some of the smaller pieces date back to the 1940s. The equipment for small batches is hardly made now, but Valerie informs me that a recent spur in interest is causing a change. In the alcove to the left are elongated bakery carts, the kind often used for cooling tray upon tray of croissants and apple danishes. Instead of pastries there are rounds, slabs, and pillowed pyramids of cheese.

Valerie is busy attaching a paddle to her silver KitchenAid. From a bag she ladles fresh chèvre into the bowl. As the paddle begins to whip the cheese, she seasons with salt. "The cheese has flavor, but really, it needs the salt." When Valerie first started experimenting the result was fresh spreadable cheese. The family gobbled it up, pressed her to make more. So she signed up for a couple of cheese classes and kept concocting at home.

Once the cheese is salted and in some cases flavored (dill and onion, chipotle chili and garlic, tomato basil, tomato jalapeño, roasted garlic, chive, Boursin, pesto) Valerie packs it into ten-pound bags. Vacuum-sealed and stored in a restaurant's freezer, the fresh cheese can last up to fourth months. In the fridge it stays fresh for three weeks. The ten-pound bags are her most popular size. Each week Valerie processes, seasons, and bags two thousand pounds of fresh goat cheese.

From start to finish chèvre takes eighteen hours to make— from udder to refrigerator bags. A four-foot-tall pasteurizer, stainless-steel and cylindrical, stoutly flanks the cool room. Pasteurizing takes only a few hours—a hundred gallon batches of goat milk are heated to 145 degrees and kept bubbling for half an hour before cooling to 75-85 degrees, the exact temperature depending on the type of cheese. Give or take, a gallon of milk transforms into a pound of cheese. In a typical week Heart Song Farm will produce two hundred pounds of cheese in assorted varieties. In an unusually good week the total rises to three hundred.

The heat flash kills bacteria residing in the milk, but also denatures the enzymes that would assist in cheese curdling. Valerie must add those back in. The milk must sit overnight after heating. Only then is it ready to be "dipped." Valerie removes the lid of the pasteurizer to reveal a yellow-white liquid—the whey; the smell of yogurt is thick in the air. Skimming this off into buckets to be fed to the goats reveals a smooth surface of pure white curd. With her spoon, Valerie dips into curd the consistency of flan. The curds are then delicately laid into cheesecloth sacks that rest, resembling beige stomachs, and into perforated cups. There they will sit for a day to drain. Soon the pockmarked curd takes on the appearance of the moon.

—m—

When Valerie first started experimenting with curds, friends shook their heads. Her initial forays into goat herding engendered similar response. "But I was looking at gourmet magazines and seeing the rise in goat cheese—just getting big in California, but not yet here. I knew if I could get in I would be on the ground floor running." Still dipping curd, Valerie shakes her head. "But, the real challenge wasn't the cheese. The real challenge was the combination of making cheese and teaching school."

For twenty years Valerie Jarvis homeschooled her ten children—preschool, elementary school, high school. Last year was the first year that she enrolled the kids in a standard school. She was burned out. How did the youngest five deal with the transition to the Gilmanton public school? "They did great. I should have set them ahead a year." In the first year Libby won awards in math, science, art and Spanish. Matt went off to college at the age of sixteen. At Norwich University in Vermont, he scored a record high at the university on the Air Force pilot exam.

Valerie initially had no intention of homeschooling her brood. "But we were sitting by the baby pool the summer Matthew was four, and there were these kids cussing like sailors. They had no respect, snatching things from others. I asked myself if this was the kind of society I was sending Matt into?" Valerie kept Matt at home that first year and taught him herself. "He did so well that first year, blossomed so much without the peer pressure, we made it a way of life."

Throughout her years of teaching, Valerie never followed one curriculum, preferring to sample, swap and switch depending on the kids' interests and passions. Sometimes too she worked with other homeschooling parents in the neighborhood, but not with any regularity. Fundamentals—math, English, writing, reading—took place in the morning, nine to twelve, often inside. In the afternoon the focus was science and history, often including field trips to battlefields, forts, museums. Valerie encouraged hands-on learning. Because she did not care to isolate her children, all ten became involved in afterschool activities at the local public school—band, soccer, gymnastics. During study time Valerie would slip out to work with the goats. Experimental cheese making occupied the only remaining available slot: midnight.

Camembert—four inches in diameter. Sainte Maure—mold ripened, ash rolled logs, six ounces Cheddesque—aged twenty-four months and more, sharp, great for grating. Miniature pyramids of Valençay—caked in salted vegetable ash and white mold. Buttons—small hardened rounds of goat cheese, smoked with applewood, bathed in wine that stains them violet, rolled in Herbs de Provence, topped with roasted red peppers. Chanson du Coeur (Song of the Heart) Blanc—mold ripened. Chanson du Coeur Noir—mold ripened and dusted in ash. Le Coeur Brise (Broken Heart)—ash on the outside and a delicate line of the same running through the core. Heart Song Salata, Heart Song Farm Feta Secco.

"Making cheese is not like following a recipe where you throw everything in and it works. You have to sense where the milk is at. I have developed that sense from years of making mistakes." Typically Valerie will age three different cheeses at one time, but even that modest number can be tricky; one has to be careful to prevent the different molds from hitchhiking to other cheese varieties. All of her more than twenty cheeses start with the same base.

Molds usually require two weeks to grow and four weeks to

mature into their peak flavor. The molded cheeses in particular are temperamental, requiring constant supervision, multiple flips and rotations to ensure an even healthy coat. When finished, they must be packaged in specialized breathable plastics. "I'm really a perfectionist," Valerie admits. "This was a real issue in the beginning. I would make a Camembert and I would throw it away if it wasn't perfectly flat. I would freak out if I found one speck of blue on a white cheese. But the chefs seemed to always love what I offered them." Typically in a week Valerie will form 125 cheeses. In the process of creation Valerie will handle each individual cheese over twenty times.

The curd ladled and set to drain, Valerie takes me out back behind the house to the paddocks. During the day the goats graze behind the farm in irregularly shaped fields denoted by electric fencing. The goats come in a forest of hues—dark brown, tawny, black and white, full white—six different breeds in all. There are Nubians with floppy ears, Alpines and Saanens with pointy upright ears, LaManchas with barely any ears. Also mixed in the herd is a lone Swiss Oberhasli. Valerie's two bucks populate a separate pen, always with a harem of nannies. There is two-year-old Dudley, a South African Boer Goat with stocky legs, a brown head, white body and a flat, wedged face. Then there is Scion, one-year-old, with black and white patches and a long nose, curled horns and a grandfatherly beard—a Billy Goat Gruff. The nannies are no longer given names. There are just too many. But Valerie still knows each individually. She distinguishes them by their udders. "You could bring me all my white goats and line them up and from looking at their udders I could tell you who was related to whom, as well as the milk production history of each."

—◆—

At Heart Song Farm home-school lessons are not limited to the U.S. Presidents and quadratic equations. "The goats teach you so much about patience, about the circle of life. The kids have seen goats being born, having sex, dying. There are no illusions about any of it … We've had the deepest conversations standing together and shoveling manure. Boys just don't sit down and tell you how they feel, but we are working and that makes it all right." With the goats, everyone helped. When the kids grew old enough, at least bigger than the goats themselves, they watered the goats and carried in the hay. The little girls always helped bottle-feed the babies; the older ones learned to dip the curd and pack the cheese. Every one learned to milk. As Valerie explains, "We had to work together as a family just to have family time."

During that first year of cheese making Valerie recalls never taking a vacation. "It's a very demanding life style–three-hundred and sixty-five days a year and it doesn't matter if it's Christmas or your birthday." Heart Song Farm has a "Cheaper by the Dozen" air to it. Remarkably though, chaos is at a minimum. What remains is a strong sense that any idea, any passion, can be pursued, and likely as not, it has been. In that first year, with nine kids and over twenty goats, Valerie contemplated, of all things, adoption. "I decided when we were done having kids we would adopt." Leanna was ten when she came to Heart Song Farm from St. Petersburg, Russia. "It was a struggle at times,"

Valerie admits. "She spoke only Russian when she first arrived." The family spoke only English. But soon everyone was speaking a fusion language—"Leannase." In more recent years Valerie's load has waned just a little. The children are growing older and at times she has hired men to help with the goats. She singles out one as a case in point. "Leon," indicating the man whom I saw earlier bottle-feeding baby goats, "is a god-send. It's hard to find people willing to do the down-to-earth work on a farm. I would adopt him if I could!"

As if her life was not complicated enough, Valerie and Bill divorced in 2007. By that point she had ten children: Matt, Mark, Hannah, Jesse, Leanna, Tabitha, Levi, Libby, Moriah, and Melody. Not to mention more than sixty goats. The farm became the family's sole support. "Other people in the business tend to think conservatively. But when you are supporting a family you have to think big." How did she manage? "I didn't sleep much."

These days Valerie can catch a little more sleep. In 2008 she met Rob Jarvis through Match.com. Within a month they were married. To add to Valerie's ten, Rob brought five children to their fold. The two youngest girls are still in school and comparable in age to Valerie's youngest. In Valerie's words, Rob has worked wonders on the farm—redesigning the feed system, the goat houses, even helping with the cheese.

Valerie never saw herself as a goat farmer, a maker of artisan cheese or mother of fifteen. In high school in Maryland she had every intention of becoming a doctor. She was a driven straight-A pre-med. "But then I worked in a physical therapy ward and was overwhelmed by the emotion of patients in so much pain."

She reconsidered her plan to attend college and moved instead to Italy, where her parents were stationed, and met Bill, who was in the Air Force at the time. "My biggest regret was leaving school. I loved school. I think that's part of the reason I was drawn to making goat cheese, getting my pilot's license, homeschooling my children. I loved the challenge of mastering something I had no exposure to or experience in."

Years ago, when Valerie was first separating curd and whey, there were fifteen small farms dipping and draining local cheese—sheep, goat and cow—in New Hampshire. By 2009 only four such farms remained, including Heart Song Farm. According to the 2007 USDA Agriculture census, New Hampshire boasted one of the largest percentages of female farmers in the whole of the United States of America. Across the country the figures keep rising; it is now estimated that fourteen percent of all farms are owned by women. "Yet still, everyone thinks you can't do it," scoffs Valerie. Of course there are limitations, she admits. "I've sat out in the yard crying because I can't lift a fence post or fix an electrical thing." What does she do? Find friends who are willing to stop by and hotwire the tractor or lend a hand with a fence pole. "I really love working for myself. If I work ten times harder I'm the one who is going to reap the benefits and not someone above me." Valerie estimates that she now produces ten thousand pounds of cheese a year. The weight of one African bull elephant in chèvre.

Valerie sells primarily to high-end chalkboard chefs—chefs who are constantly changing their menus, drawing inspiration from what she has to offer on any given day. Forty-five restaurants spread across New Hampshire and Maine dice, slice and crumble her chèvre over mesclun salads and hearth pizzas, or lay her cheese diagonal on wood boards beside berry compotes. Chefs across the two states are partial to blue cheeses. Valençay is favored—Valerie alternates batches of Valençay (twelve pyramids per batch) and Camembert, Valençay and Sainte Maure. Each year she experiments with a new recipe. The Heart Song Farm Feta Secco arose out of the naggings of a particular chef's desire for feta. "I didn't want to use lipase (a pancreatic enzyme used for coagulation) because in my opinion it makes the cheese smell of dirty feet." She left it out, created a batch and brought it to the chef, who loved it. "Every chef has their favorite cheese, but they also want to be the cool kid on the block with the new cheese." Restaurants buy small and often.

"I was such a nervous wreck when I first started bringing my cheeses to chefs. This was my art and I was walking in and saying, 'Do you like my art?' I took everything so personally." These days Valerie no longer goes looking for business. Chefs talk to each other, sharing tips on favorite suppliers. When one chef leaves a restaurant, they still want her cheese at their next kitchen. "Cheese making has personally changed my life. Now I walk into a kitchen and say, 'Hey, I've got something you might want to try.'"

Valerie hopes to expand, but she is not sure the farm can support any more goats. Money is in the molds and in retail. Pound for pound, aged varieties sell for double the price. Selling retail rather than to restaurants brings similarly higher returns. Fresh cheese sells for $10 per pound at a restaurant, $16 at a retail outlet, $22 at a farmer's market. "I didn't know what to expect when I first started, but I like the creative side of cheese making, it keeps me interested. For me, cheese is more of an art form than just a product. But when I first started it was hard to tell if I was doing it right. I hadn't eaten much goat cheese, I never ate it as a kid. All I knew was Kraft."

In the house, the whole family eats goat cheese. Valerie is partial to the buttons—applewood smoked. Occasionally she will allow herself a Valençay: "I don't let myself eat them often; they are just too good." We are walking back up through the tall grass toward the house. The goats crane their necks at our departure. The house is quieter now. The older children have grown up and spread across the country, in one case the globe. Matt, Mark, Hannah and Jessie are all married. Matt is a youth pastor, Mark a mission-school director, Hannah is raising two sons of her own, Jessie is studying the Bible in Johannesburg, South Africa. When they can, they return to the farm, often on the Fourth of July, which coincides with Valerie's birthday. Valerie stops in the dirt driveway, taking in the barn, the house, the fields. "I've been raising kids for a long time. At some point though, they have to find their own way."

Gilman Town

IN MAY OF 1727, a charter was granted. The giver: Colonial Governor John Wentworth. The recipient: one hundred and seventy-seven defenders of England. The gift: 83,500 acres of central New Hampshire. Twenty-four of the crowd bore the same surname. Peter Gilman, Daniel Gilman, Andrew Gilman, Nathaniel Gilman, Nehemiah Gilman. There were two John Gilmans, one Josiah Gilman, Joseph Gilman, Jonathan Gilman, John Gilman Jr. and a Jeremiah Gilman. Three Nicholas Gilmans, a Sr., a Jr. and a 3rd. An Edward Gilman Jr., a Nathaniel Gilman Jr., a Samuel Gilman III. Trueworthy Gilman, Caleb Gilman, Robert Gilman, Thomas Gilman, Samuel Gilman and Captain John Gilman. The town was christened Gilmantown, condensed with time to Gilmanton.

Gilmantown, inked on parchment in 1727, remained for years nothing more than lines on a map. The original charter demanded of the town each year a pound of flax and all the mast trees desired by His Majesty's Navy. It required the construction of seventy dwellings, each with tended pastures, and demanded that the land be cultivated within three years. Threats by Winnipesaukee tribesmen dissuaded settlers for over thirty.

Snowshoes were the first settlers' means of transportation onto Gilmanton soil. A frost-chapped Benjamin and Hannah Mudgett set out from Epsom on the morning of Boxing Day, 1761. They spent the night, after traversing twelve snow-strewn miles, as the sole settlers of a town equal in size to the Caribbean country of Grenada. The winter snow fell deep, capable of covering completely a standing man. In subsequent years, low temperatures formed crusts of colossal strength, a layer of frozen crystal strong enough to bear the weight of entire ox teams. The Mudgetts did not remain alone long; they were followed shortly by a brother, John Mudgett, and his wife, and a Mr. and Mrs. Orlando Weed. More and more came, Gilmanton growing name by name. By 1834, the year Hannah Mudgett expired at the age of ninety-five, outliving her husband by twenty-seven years, her town of two had blossomed to nearly 3,500.

July

The storm came on suddenly—sun and blue skies, and then wind and rain and lightning—like a switch being flicked. Storms do that in July. They come hurtling down the road, skirts flying, and leave everything dripping and steaming. On this particular afternoon the sky remained light despite the downpour. I went out to dance in the rain. I spun in circles until I grew dizzy and then lay face upturned to catch raindrops, staying till my whole body was soaked save for the small of my back. Looking skyward I was perplexed to find a cascade of tattered oak leaves spinning wildly from high up in the heavens. Hours later I discovered that the oak leaves were rent from their branches in a tornado that jig-sawed its way just four miles from the Iron Works. Tornadoes are not common here.

A long time ago we canoed down the Suncook on the heels of a storm. The sky had cleared and we saw two paddlers pass along our stretch of river, portaging over the dam. Our family decided to follow suit and so the five of us lugged our canoe down to the river, climbed in and set off. The adventure was short-lived and ill-fated. Just below the apple orchard, barely a turn below where we put in, a downed pine barricaded the river's width. The Suncook was swollen and temperamental and it slammed our canoe broadside against the trunk. Gasping and sputtering we clutched at the rim of our upside-down canoe and at the pine branches. We swam to shore before attempting to pry our canoe free. But the current was powerful and the river possessive. We were forced to leave it wedged against the pine for an entire month before the river's swell subsided.

July is hot, wet and overrun with weeds. Tomatoes blush and radishes grow rotund. There are raspberries and blueberries and, in late July, wild blueberries. Rain is the lead player. Too much, and the ground grows waterlogged and vegetables rot from the roots. Too little, and we rig sprinkler systems and pull out watering cans and even then leaves wilt and stalks shrivel over as if plagued by osteoporosis. In either extreme it is only the weeds that persist.

July days become filled with serendipitous adventures. In the heat I put off contemplating and cataloging, and just live day-to-day, story-to-story. These mid-summer days are long and so tangled in each other that I abandon time altogether. I discard the watches that keep me in check during the rest of the year. Cell phones fail to locate signals in the Iron Works and with little regret I set mine aside. Time expands, making days pliant. The sun is up early, burning the morning mist, and in the evening, the sun drags its feet in the sky, slouching into lingering dusk. Darkness brings with it winking fireflies and fluttering bats.

Served with a Prayer

AT 9:30 THE CROWDS congeal, bright in patriotic hues, with still a half hour to wait. A line of cars, parked along Route 140, stretches past the bridge, a house, another house and ten birdhouses. The birdhouses float eight feet high on graying bedposts: narrow tin-roofed red barns, squat green and white log cabins, green gabled colonials, abstracted miniature replicas of century old homes—grayed wood, red tin, turquoise shutters. Dodge Caravans, Honda Civics, Ford pickups trim Route 140 up past a house mail-ordered from Sears Roebuck seventy years previous and assembled like Playmobil pieces.

Back amongst the crowd, Route 140 skips across Province Road as it sweeps steeply down Lamprey Hill and into the center of Gilmanton Four Corners before rising up again to crest Peaks Hill. People claim front-row spots, flanking the road. Some have hauled lawn chairs. I choose to sit right down along the embankment of Town Hall, on the grassy rise before the library.

A two-room squat structure, the library was once a tailor

shop; a hatter shop; a court room; a printing office; the home of a Mr. Blodgett called "Commodore" by neighbors; a school that taught, among other things, French, and, most prominently, a cobbler's workshop. The weary shoemaker Ira Pennock is immortalized in an ochre painting. Straddling a wood bench, he inspects a child's laced boot. Beside him stands a nine-year-old girl, Emma Wight, curly haired and angelic. Below, the caption: "What does your mother think I can do with this?" The painting was once used to market shoes across America, but the cobbler shop has long since closed, the child grown and married to an Amos Price from Gilmanton Iron Works. The library door, large, white and bowed, as if it were a stomach engorged, was once so intriguing that it engendered investigation in *The Laconia Democrat* in 1880:

> There is a great curiosity in town to know the why and wherefore that the door in Mr. Pennock's shoe-shop will invariably jam your heel when closing after you? And why should a door bulge in the upright center, unless for the aforesaid jam behind?

The *Democrat* reports that the door was the sole remnant of another house consigned to flames, whose porch bulged in a similar radius. The door was once considered oddity enough for submission to a proposed World's Fair of the late eighteen hundreds, halfway around the globe in Honolulu. However, when it was discovered that King Kalākaua would never appreciate the eccentricity, because he never shut doors himself, the idea was discarded. The door remained in Gilmanton.

Kids dash back and forth into the road, checking and recheck-
ing the hill, still silent, for signs of the parade. Some of the more
prepared have brought caps or donned loose clothing with large
pockets for stuffing candy. Everyone knows someone, often
many someones, in the crowd.

Past Centre Congregational Church—high, steepled, constructed in 1826—the parade will trot. No one can recall the
inaugural date of the parade—newspaper advertisements speak
of it as far back as the 1870s. Back then there used to be picnics at
Rocky Pond, fireworks at Sunset Rock. At midnight the church
bell would ring, accompanied by the raucous howling of much
frowned-upon carousers.

Across the way, the parade will pass the tall, flat façade of
Number 500. Thick, with mismatched windows, the house sits
sullenly, twice foreclosed within the past decade. I have explored
the home just once, led through the derelict homestead by a
realtor who was not keen to market its connection to Herman
Webster Mudgett, America's first serial killer.

Mudgett discarded his given name when he moved to Chicago
in the mid-1880s, where he carried out most of his murders. He
was a direct descendant of the Mudgetts who settled Gilmanton,
but that did not tie him to the land. As a young man he quit
his job teaching across the road at the Academy and left for the
Midwest. Graduated from the University of Michigan and newly
registered as a doctor, Mudgett bought black bowlers and grew
a glossy handlebar mustache to attract the ladies. He completed
his transformation by fashioning a new name for himself: Dr.
Henry Howard Holmes. H. H. Holmes for short. Decades later,

the public would take to calling him the "Torture Doctor."

Inside Number 500, there is an overenthusiastic collection of staircases, scratched and warped glass, and wide-beamed floorboards set akimbo. If I had carried a marble with me I could have placed it at one end of the house and watched it roll and roll and roll. In Chicago, Mudgett constructed a labyrinth of a castle reportedly modeled on the twisted maze of Number 500. By the end of his life, Mudgett would admit to torturing and murdering a total of twenty-seven people—predominantly young women. Skeletal remains in his Chicago mansion, partially burned, acid-bleached, suggested a tally closer to two hundred.

Just below the point of Number 500's roof, a solitary window throws light into a lonely white-washed cell. The room is stark with missing floorboards. I have peered up at this room from the outside and I timidly explored its interior, all the while imagining how a century and a half ago, a disobedient Mudgett spent hours locked in this attic as punishment.

Gilmanton's younger generation knows little of the notorious history of this house. On this sunny July morning, the parade will pass in front of Number 500 without acknowledgment, continuing its march down the hill.

—⚬—

Farther along, the parade will pass alongside the green-shuttered Temperance Tavern. It was founded as a spirit-selling tavern in 1793, but the temperance movement across New Hampshire plugged the flow less than twenty years later. Liquor bottles were emptied to make way for sacks of envelopes and drawers of stamps: a bar turned post office. The Tavern is now a private home, but over the centuries, it has housed Academy students, circuit judges, Concord stage coach passengers, and Freemasons. The master bedroom was dubbed Monticello Lodge in 1828. Along the walls are the stenciled remnants of carpenters' compasses and triangular trees.

It is 9:40 a.m. and farther up Province Road, the parade is amassing at the corner of High Street. Six Army vets, uniforms starched, skin wrinkled, mill below a branching pine. Returned from Vietnam, Korea, Europe, the men no longer live in Gilmanton, yet faithfully they return every year for the parade. Two flags—America's and New Hampshire's—lean furled against a tree trunk, accompanied by two antique rifles. The vets stand chatting with a woman trailing two girls and two sheep in tow. The sheep are named Killy and Kera, black-faced with cream-colored coats cropped close. A Cub Scout troop has abandoned its homemade cardboard boats and race cars. In groups they fiddle with gaudy medals pinned high on their chests, poke at a pug puppy, poke at each other. A red Ford pickup is strapped to their float—toting a nature scene complete with a foam profile of the Old Man in the Mountain, fake pumpkins and a real stuffed doe. The boys dress in Scout attire—beige shorts, navy button downs, colored bandanas, and caps—orange for tiger scout, yellow for wolf scout, light blue for bear scout. Close behind is a "Think Green" float; the creators are the Cub Scouts' sisters. Giggling girls, partially camouflaged in green T-shirts with "recycle" triangles sketched in black Sharpie, pose for a picture, crouching next to their green construction. A woman issues instructions on the proper protocol for candy throwing: "Toss the candy gently; we don't want anyone getting hurt."

Walking past a collection of kids next to patriotic bikes decked out in tinsel, ribbons, streamers and crepe paper, I am waylaid by a five-foot bottle of Crest mouthwash. "Would you like some dental floss?" I follow the antiseptic girl, Callie, to an oversized collection of dental products. The youngest, Katie, is dressed like the boxes of floss I've just been given; their uncle is dressed as a dentist. At 14, Callie is the talkative one. The idea, she explains, came from Uncle Tibbs. "He thought there was too much candy at the parade." Each year the family selects a different theme: characters from *Lemony Snicket* and *Charlotte's Web*, people from 1904, library gnomes, and, once, a schoolhouse complete with a walking chalkboard. Callie had no intention of marching this year. Few fourteen-year-olds would willingly parade past the entire town resembling a five-foot bottle of mouthwash. "I got talked into it last night ... it's a little embarrassing," she smiles ruefully.

Farther on is a line of antique cars. Anyone is allowed to ride in the parade: all one must do is show up on time, and many dust off cars for the occasion. A boney, white-haired man leans out of a turquoise hot rod. Proudly he describes how he converted the car three years earlier from a S-10 pickup. A man buffs the gleaming hubcaps of a '49 Chevrolet deluxe convertible; American flags are taped to the windshield and a candy-filled wicker basket rests between the seats. A woman with pale, frizzy hair chronicles the restoration of her 1956 Thunderbird. "It sat in a field for seventeen years." It took her husband five years to

restore. "There were rats!" She thrusts a glossy photo at me, gnawed leather seats, weeds woven through the steering wheel. Next—a 1962 Corvette, bright red. This will be the steel-haired driver's fourth year in the parade, he tells me. He drives the low rider as often as he can, but has only a limited number of places to go. He adds wistfully, "you can only get the newspaper once a day."

Somewhere near the front a horn sounds. Men and women mount trucks and drop cross-legged onto floats. The black-faced sheep clip-clop past, green fair ribbons twirling from woolen necks. Still farther up Province Road the town fire engines have arrived. A Navy vet, retired in '93, surveys the motley assembly of paraders critically. "We should probably start this thing up."

Walking back down toward the village center, I pass parade-goers arranged in swaths along the slope. Twirling paper flags bat at the morning breeze. A fire engine sounds, the flags cease spinning, necks crane and kids scurry back to the road's edge. I tuck myself between families crowded in front of the Academy, built first as a school house in 1793 when tuition was a dollar a term, but since burned to the grass twice (and rebuilt twice). A century ago it held balls and townwide suppers on July Fourth; now it functions as Town Hall. From behind someone calls my name. Turning, I find Larry Frates, a neighbor in the Iron Works who, for several summers, led week-long theater camps, staging plays with the local kids. I played an evil queen and, once, a chicken. We exchange greetings. "You know I have pictures I need to give you from when you were little." I was not a very attractive chicken, lots of leg and scraggly yellow. "But maybe I'll save them for some inopportune time."

After the parade there is always a fair, held on the lawn in front of the Academy. Antique tables show off rusty flour sieves, stained fur-lined veils, and Boston Celtics license plates. A tent stand exhibits vintage hats, vintage jewelry, and, in one corner, hand-knit infant caps like woolen strawberries—red with protruding green tops. Near the Moon Bounce, which bobs like Jell-O from the kids within, there is a table with Fourth of July paraphernalia: flags, candy canes, blow-up balls, bubbles, bracelets. Gray shirts, white shirts, and navy shirts read: "Gilmanton Corners 4th of July, Coming together to celebrate" and "4th of July, Gilmanton NH, incorporated 1727." A crotchety woman selling cheap plastic toys scolds wandering hands grasping at water guns, disappearing ink, handcuffs, stink bombs, bomb bags, poppers, parasols. The summer library is having a book sale. The Gilmanton Youth Organization is grilling hotdogs ($1) and burgers ($2). Teenage girls shovel Snow Cones: grape, cherry, strawberry, tangerine and island ice ($1.50 a cup.) The Gilmanton Year Round Library is raising money to continue construction, selling tote bags, sweatshirts and onesies; they also have handmade soap, book plates, and cookbooks with resident recipes. A blue and white quilt lies draped across a card table: first prize for the winner of the Old Home Day raffle.

The fair's main event is not on the Academy's green, but in the basement of Centre Church. Large block print signs proclaim: "Strawberry Shortcake Festival, Under Church." "Fabulous Strawberry Shortcake! Homemade Biscuits! Real Whip Cream! Hand picked Berries! 5 dollars—always sold out!" "Strawberry Shortcake. Best bargain of all. Served with a prayer."

The past quarter-century has been rich with biscuits, cream, and berries, but the festival has only been recently incorporated into the Fourth of July festivities; it used to be held a week prior. The pastor reckons forty churchgoers contribute by picking 70 pounds of berries, buying 15 quarts of heavy cream, hulling, creaming, and baking biscuits. The previous night, the pastor herself baked five dozen biscuits.

I skirt past a pair of wispy haired women, backs bent and clutching canes. Past a small girl in white and red polka dots, parents trailing. "You almost look like a shortcake," the mother coos. The line for shortcake seeps into three corners of the cavernous church basement, fully encircling elderly couples already consuming cake, chairs drawn close, bowls and napkins resting on a strawberry print tablecloth. Assembled shortcakes go on sale at 10:30 sharp, but the pastor assures me there are some who don't bother with the parade and are in line by 10. I am lucky. I arrive in time to meet my younger brother, Styrofoam bowl in hand, biscuits and strawberries peeking out from beneath cream. He is kind enough to share his spoon. By the end of the day, the women manning the kitchen will have composed two hundred bowls of shortcake.

—⁓—

But before shortcakes and snow cones, before burgers are slapped on the grill, there is the parade. From behind the bend, sirens firework through the hot morning air, a police car rolls down the hill, and an American flag ripples past the tree line. Solemn and stiff-legged, the six vets march down in military regalia, rifles resting on shoulders. Applause rises with the heat along the road.

The Scouts are next, navigating their cardboard sailboats and race cars at waist height and chucking candy into the crowd. Peppermints, Atomic Fireballs, Tootsie Rolls, Hershey Kisses, SweeTarts, Smarties, Dum Dums. Callie and her dental crew skip by, tossing floss. One lands amidst a collection of older parade goers, "Ooooo," they lean over, excited. The turquoise hot rod rolls by, the driver tossing candy; Larry Frates tosses back catcalls. There is a procession of antique cars—some buffed to a polish, others shedding paint and shuddering. An upright revolver stands as bonnet ornament on an old red Ford. The driver presses a button; the gun shoots smoke.

The line of tractors follows. A rusted red one is driven by a blond boy with a sheepish grin, dragging a sand pit complete with toy pickup trucks. An Allis-Chalmers drags another tractor, a glossy green John Deere rumbles by, then another, and another. Next a Farmall 656 diesel, big back wheels and a tall narrow radiator in bright red, a 1066 International with a two-foot high exhaust pipe standing erect in front of the windshield. "Gun the engine!" a man yells. The driver obliges; the pipe belches black smoke. Hand-drawn memorials to "Old Tom Smithers" decorate the tractors. Tom Smithers, not long dead at age eighty, was a road agent and never missed a parade and a chance to show off his collection of antique tractors.

Each year prizes are awarded: most original, most beautiful, funniest, best of the antiques and Judge's Choice. A decade back, Larry conducted a military precision marching brigade of fifteen flamboyantly attired lawn chair-toting men and women. They cranked chairs, rippled them for the wave, the snake and the grand march. Their uniform: Bermuda shorts, Hawaiian shirts, and neon plastic shades. Practice began fifteen minutes before the performance. The brigade won the prize for funniest entry two years running. Ninety years ago a stagecoach drawn by four horses, their color unrecorded, won the grand prize. A special ribbon was once awarded to a girl who led her pet Jersey heifer down the road, both dressed in peonies for the occasion.

Until last year, there was an old, full-bellied man with a fluffy white beard, tri-cornered hat and red suspenders, who drove a pair of gigantic oxen pulling a blue cart and barrel hung with a sixteen-star US flag. There was a one-man band—tall, thin, with a large wooden drum for a belly, a harmonica for lips. In

1913 three men paraded as President Taft, President Wilson and Colonel Roosevelt. They rigged up a wagon and attached antlers to their horse—their own personal Bull Moose.

A 1931 Model A Ford, black and red with wooden doors passes by. A large gap follows before the next float passes. Ahead of the church's float walks a short woman in a strawberry print dress, the town pastor. Behind her, the Gilmanton Highway Department, in its entirety, rolls big-wheeled down the road. Massive orange caterpillar trucks, red Fords, dump trucks, backhoes. A little boy exuberantly chucks toffees like torpedoes into the crowd. Two horses are next; they prance ahead of the fire engines. Kids clap sticky hands to their ears; so do some adults. The fire engines, sirens yelling, lights flashing, mark the end of the parade. It is 10:25. The crowd cheers, flags whipping wildly along both sides of the road. The parade tails down past the Tavern, the library, and the corner store. People stream over to the fair, to tables of antiques, face painting, book sales, and burgers. Others head straight for shortcake. Back on the road, two boys have clambered onto the asphalt; they run up and down, bent double, scavenging for sweets.

Raking for Berries

ANDY GEDDES DREAMS about blueberries. July and August are ripe with nightmares, "I see little blue dots whenever I close my eyes." Andy is fifteen and the youngest of the grandkids on the family's wild blueberry farm. "I'm the last one my uncle Duncan has got to trap into work." At three, Andy was commissioned as a sticker boy, paid to decorate pints and quarts with oval orange stickers: "Wild." Other times, he was commissioned to play outdoors. "I was actually paid to go away!" Two dollars an hour, as he recalls. These days, Andy no longer earns money through his absence; instead he is paid to remain in the barn sorting berries. Four years ago, he added raking berries to his repertoire.

The sun is wilting in an afternoon sky, but Andy is in the cool of the barn sorting. Near the door, stacked wood boxes loom, shaggy with twigs, leaves, and blue rounds the size of Dippin' Dots ice cream. Wild low-bush blueberries are nothing like their high-bush, marble-sized relatives. They are smaller and vastly harder to pick and sort, but much sweeter. Andy balances a wooden crate atop the sorting machine, which is a series of criss-crossing conveyer belts that resembles a mechanized marble run.

In an indigo trickle, blueberries stream from between Andy's fingers, tumbling backward down a foot-long belt. A fan whacks air at leaves, twigs, and pinprick green fruit, sending them on home-run hits over the ramp to fall down, down into a pink plastic tub. Pig berries. The family no longer keeps pigs, but the neighborhood swine hardly complain. Berries that bypass the windy ride catch a second shuttle, a perpendicularly angled belt that sends them rolling below the fan in zigzags. Next comes a wide belt, four feet across, slow and shallow. Clumps—ripe berries that stubbornly have remained in triplets, quadruplets, sextets—come to a halt. They never make the finish line. The conveyer belt churns steadily sideways, until it turns under itself and the clumps plummet into three wooden crates. The crated berries are distilled into locally brewed blueberry soda or, as happened the previous year, into blueberry wine.

Berries that tumble past the fan and clump extractor are almost home free, but not quite. A final belt remains, horizontal, five feet long. Three teens sit huddled along its length. Shoulders hunched, heads bent, hands glide across the stained surface like gulls above the surf and then dive. Fingers pinch, rise again, a berry suspended—green or red or oozing juice. Rejects are dropped into sagging green quarts. Purple stained fingertips earn five dollars an hour the first year. Somewhere between the second and third year, the wage grows to a plump eight.

Grace has sorted blueberries since she was ten. She is nineteen now. "We didn't want to hire you at first," adds Barbara, who supervises the barn (a Geddes by marriage). "You were too young." Barely five feet, Grace wears blond, braided pigtails, shoulder length. Grace lives at the bottom of the hill and has known the Geddes her entire life. Courtney, hunched near the end of the conveyer belt, also lives along Geddes Road, but this is only her third year sorting. Fluorescent pink bangs erupt out of dyed black hair; Courtney's shoelaces mimic her hair with added twists of green. John sits farther back along the belt, curly haired and silent. It is only his second day on the job. Yesterday, he tried to rake with little success. "I tried raking one summer," Grace tells me. "Me and four other girls decided to give it a go … it took five of us an hour to rake a single box."

Swathed in plastic and belted with a rubber band, the pint is nestled snug in a cardboard flat. Tonight Duncan will play chauffeur to ninety flats of wild blueberries, each weighing approximately eighty pounds. Duncan's wife Barbara is thirty-five, long-faced and sun-weathered. She stands behind the white-topped table, looking out over berries, a naked bulb and florescent rods overhead.

Last year the wide-beamed barn room was only half the size, a wall slicing down the middle. Before renovations, filled pints were balanced on beams over a dirt floor. The newly finished wood flooring supports whole cities of stacked blueberry box skyscrapers. Empty flats form a great wall of cardboard in front of the barn's old wooden one. Erected in the early 1900s, the barn is white with green shutters, and crowned with a hand-painted sign nailed over the door: "Fresh Native Blueberries."

On Wednesdays the berries are brought to Chelsea's Wholesale

Market near Boston. Blueberries picked on Wednesday and Thursday are distributed to farmers' markets between here and Salem, Massachusetts. Friday's fruit is more leniently selected, relegated to twenty-pound freezer boxes sold locally. Each summer, our family brings home two twenty-pounders to turn into jam, pies, cobblers, sodas, smoothies, sorbets, ice cream. When we collect our prize, there is always a rush of hands, digging deep and emerging with glistening heaps of berries quickly ferried to waiting mouths.

Andy can't stand to eat blueberries. A grimace grows on his round face. "Blueberries are our job; it would feel weird to eat them," Grace elaborates. Two weeks of blue orbs, green orbs, purple orbs, an endless procession of fruit seven hours a day, five days a week is enough to make all of them blanch at the sight of anything small and indigo. Grace remembers one "freaky" year where the weather kept blueberries on the bushes straight through to October. "I had to come in and work nights!" The kids sorting blueberries usually work just one shift, day (8 a.m. to 4 p.m.) or night (7 p.m. to 9 p.m.). Rain requires a complete readjustment of the week. Wet berries cannot be raked.

Once all of the sorting occurred at night, when the family only had a small portion of the conveyer belt marble run. The fan would disentangle twigs, leaves, and immature fruit but there was no belt to sort out clumps, and no horizontal belt to ensure easy sorting. Before hiring local kids, the family would sort through the berries by hand, tossing a green one here, a clump there. They worked outside under lights, bugs waltzing wildly in the glow. Andy steps down from the fan, the crate empty. In

the last day, they have sorted ninety-two wooden crates. I take
a vote. In the barn, the tally is unanimous—blueberries are not
for eating.

—m—

I am off to Geddes farm, a flaxen sun winking, just as tired, between white pines. Morning roll call for blueberry raking is at
eight a.m. and I have promised to be prompt. I arrive at 7:30. The
yard is still, in the way mornings are before a hot day. Only spar-
rows have preceded my arrival. I call into the silent barn; the
sorting machine is shadowed—it gets to sleep in till nine. From
the depths of the house, a voice answers. I enter to find an old
woman, the late David Sr.'s wife Anna, presiding at the kitchen
table. Anna sits, robed in blue cotton, a cigarette caught between
pointed and knobbled fingers, nails painted pink.

Anna is small, but at the table she is the grand matron. Her tones are bleached—hair, skin, eyes, all look as if their color has seeped out from numerous washings. When she laughs, the sound crackles. I'm invited to sit. While I wait, she leads the conversation, holding forth on the humming birds that favor her feeder, and on country dances—particularly the one in which she met her late husband. Anna's domain is the sorting barn; Duncan (like Dave before him) oversees the fields. When it comes to sales, Duncan manages market patrons throughout New Hampshire and Massachusetts, while Anna commands a legion of local blueberry lovers who are partial to the twenty-pound packages. I ask her if she eats the blueberries. "I don't touch the blueberries till November; then I'll make a few pies for Thanksgiving."

Duncan lumbers into the kitchen at 8:30. His face is round, his nose large, his graying beard kept short. Dark eyes sharp under a red baseball cap. His arrival is the signal to depart for the fields. I wave to Anna, now on her third cigarette, and traipse outside. Boys have accumulated under a large maple, seven in all. Boys stream out of the shade, engulfing the sides of a dented pickup truck, forest green with bruises of lighter green spray paint. I sink down into the passenger seat—the coils having long since lost their spring. Duncan slides behind the wheel; we are off.

Duncan is wide-eyed and talkative. No one would suspect him of just coming off a round trip to Chelsea Market—ninety miles and back. "Staying awake is easy," he assures me. "I would have a harder time if it was late afternoon." Not that he slept the previous afternoon. Duncan's schedule yesterday as he tells it: raked with the boys all morning, helped haul horse manure (part of his

self-employed trucking job), come evening assisted berry sorting in the barn and stacked the truck high with blueberry flats. At 10 p.m., he ate dinner. From 11:30 to midnight, Duncan took a nap.

In the midst of blueberry season, Duncan drives weekly to Chelsea. He sells his berries wholesale to the New England Produce Center at one a.m., two a.m., and three a.m. By four, the farmers are supposed to have unloaded their produce, received their checks, and shifted their trucks into gear. But Duncan likes to linger. After selling his berries, he wanders away for an hour (perhaps marketing maple syrup, which he boils in April) before returning to the berry buyers. Buyers typically pay $4.75 per pint and $6.20 per quart. (The easier-to-pick high-bush blueberries are half the price in markets.) Duncan swears he is not tempted to even glance at the price his berries are resold for; but by appearing to do so, he swears he keeps the buyers honest.

Shoppers will sometimes approach him in the market offering to buy direct, but despite the higher profits proposed, Duncan declines. Duncan relies upon the middlemen to buy in bulk. "It's all about fair play."

If Duncan ever does grow sleepy on the drive, he stops and takes a couple laps around the truck. Sometimes his driving is leisurely, coffee on the way down, breakfast on the way back—often at a particular diner in Epsom. Other times he "shoots down and back" in under three and a half hours.

Despite the early morning pilgrimage, today is just another workday and Duncan has no intention of altering his routine simply because he has hardly slept within the past twenty-four hours. The truck swings right at the fork and we rollercoaster through the woods, up and down dirt roads, the truck jittering in an over-caffeinated sort of way. We swerve to the left, out of the trees, climb steeply up a meadow, painting the tires blue with squished berries. Duncan parks halfway up and boys tumble out, wooden boxes in hand. Rakes are distributed —dulled metal, a cross between a dustpan and a long-toothed comb. Blueberry bushes are everywhere—the ground a two-tone Jackson Pollock: blue on green. Stepping on blueberries is inevitable. Leaves and twigs crunch underfoot, pop back up, and purple skins burst like fireworks on my toes. The air smells of sweet ferns and blueberry syrup.

Duncan stands squarely, ringed by heavy-eyed boys, all thinner and most taller than he. He doles out reprimands for yesterday's picking. "Yesterday's berries were wet." Buyers desire dry berries with powdery white coats. Punctured berries leak juice, turning the skins slick. "If I can't sell them, I can't pay for them." Duncan does not yell. Yelling is unnecessary; his solemn demeanor is goad enough. The boys examine the rubber of their shoes and offer no excuses.

Dismissed, boys spread out in lanes, five feet apart, delineated by neon ribbons of pink, yellow, and green. Duncan strolls among them, offering more precise instructions. "Just run your rake slowly and carefully, low to the ground and make sure you get them all ... start where the berries begin, don't skip berries." When blueberry season comes, Duncan need not look for rakers; wannabe rakers come looking for him. The hours are eight a.m. to noon, an hour for lunch, and another three hours in the afternoon. Rakers earn two dollars for every wooden crate filled. A swift raker can sweep seventy dollars in a day. Most rake in twenty-five. "All set, Matt?" Wide-eyed behind glasses and scrawny, Matt looks out of place among the long-limbed adolescents. Duncan points him in the direction of a row resembling chickenpox gone blue.

Duncan retraces his steps between beech saplings. "I'm really hard and fussy with these kids," he admits, his tone unabashed. "I want all the berries I can." Duncan's fastidiousness seems justified. Berries knocked to the ground lead to maggot worms and fungus. At market, certain buyers won't take anyone's berries but his. Duncan demands quality with his boys and high prices with his buyers. Out in the field, Duncan can be found bent double, rake clasped loosely in hand. Duncan never brings a box. He plucks berries skirting trees and lacing stone walls— areas requiring a knowledgeable rake and a firm hand. Once full,

Duncan empties his rake into a boy's crate. With a sigh, he admits: "I like to help them out."

Nearby, a gunshot bursts through the underlining hum of field crickets. I jump. Duncan laughs, his bristles quivering. He gestures to a scraggly maple at the far end of the field. The tree wears a chain necklace sporting what looks like a heavy-duty water-gun, long-nozzled and metal. The water gun is in fact a sound cannon—a Thunderbird Scare-Away noisemaker, powered by propane and costing four hundred dollars. Duncan has two, one at each field. Combined they fire a belch that ricochets off trees every ten minutes, twenty-four hours a day. Other farmers employ chemicals and traps to thwart hungry birds, deer and bears, but then the animals have to be relocated or killed. The cannon succeeds by keeping uninvited guests nervous; who could enjoy a meal with such unpleasant dinner partners? They move on quickly. Duncan bought the cannons over twenty-five years ago. In that time he has entertained numerous visits from police responding to noise complaints lodged by neighbors who wish not to have time shattered into ten-minute increments. But some neighbors are disappointed if they don't hear the cannons. "When they do, they know it's blueberry season."

The blueberry fields and Duncan are close in age, and both have grown with time. Initially only a patch at the woods was cleared for berries. Duncan waves in the direction of the barn. Just out of high school in 1975, Duncan logged the woods with his father, and became enthralled with working the land. Clearing, over numerous years, has created two fields and thirty acres of blueberries, a hefty sixty-five tons a season. Why did his father first grow blueberries? "Beats the hell out of me!"

Duncan leads me up past the boys, bent with backs glistening, up past the truck and the stone wall where Duncan remembers having his last good chat with his father before he died. Up, up, up to the shoulder of the field where the treetops drop away and mountains pierce the horizon. Duncan singles out one in particular, a peak nicknamed Blueberry Mountain. It was on those slopes where Dave, Sr. learned to rake berries in the 1950s. The prodigious summit is responsible for not only the Geddes farm, but for almost all the other small wild blueberry farms in the area—once, thirteen in all. "Don't try making a living off this," Duncan intones. "A true farmer can't explain why he farms." The story goes that a vengeful neighbor attempted to burn two nearby homes. He burned the homes, along with the entire mountain. The following year, the slopes were swathed in blueberry bushes. Wild blueberry farms have sprouted along Gilmanton hillsides ever since.

Blueberry fields must be burned. Without fire, secession takes control, beeches and pines stealing sunlight from the berries. Duncan's fields are on a two-year rotation: each spring fifteen acres go up in flames. Hay grown and harvested by Duncan is blown on the doomed field in autumn. A matted golden blanket over winter becomes a copper blaze in early spring. By late autumn, new sprouts create a foot high emerald carpet.

High on the hill, Duncan finds a seat amongst the newly sprouting blueberry bushes. I follow suit, as does the large dog that Duncan lovingly calls Jughead. Blaming bad knees for his need to sit, he offers: "A couple of years ago I was run over by a tractor." With only a little cajoling, he relates the saga: How

Duncan was off to bale hay; how, on remembering a forgotten item, he jumped down from the tractor, which proceeded to roll away down the hill without him; how he chased it through the field, and tried to jump on it and divert it from a collision course with a fence; how he mistimed his jump and had his knee caps splintered; and how, while lying in the field unable to move, he kept repeating "Don't call an ambulance, I don't need an ambulance." He pauses, staring out at the field, a piece of grass bobbing between his lips, "It was a heavy tractor."

Knees are not the only casualty Duncan has sustained. He ticks them off on short, fleshy fingers. First finger: "When I was seven my pant leg caught on fire while I was helping my dad burn the blueberry bushes." He pulls up the leg of his pant to show a web of skin grafts. Second finger: "When I was fifteen I nearly sliced off my finger chopping wood in the yard." He waggles his extended pointer at me ornamented with a scar shaped like a ring. First thing he did was calmly inform his grandmother that he had a finger hanging on by skin only. Third finger: he holds up the backside of his left hand whose knuckles were rasped by a chain saw when he was nineteen. Finger four goes to bone spurs in neck and feet; finger five to thrice torn and operated on shoulders. Twenty years ago, doctors asked if he wished to be listed as disabled for social security benefits. He declined. "What would I do then?" When Duncan goes home at night, he ices everything.

—⟋⟍—

Today, I am to receive a lesson in blueberry raking. First Duncan selects a rake. A venerable tool with a polished wooden handle, nearly silky from years of use, it is one of two remaining original rakes. Blueberry rakes are as varied in shape, size, and personality. Short bodied rakes, fifteen inches long with thick waists and elongated teeth. Long and lean rakes, narrow bellied, stretching two feet long with stubby incisors. There are wood handles and metal handles, aluminum rakes, shiny silver rakes that blacken hands, and aged tin rakes, blotchy-skinned with indistinct shades of dark. Some rakes can be trusted with berries in any condition; others are more finicky and are only employed when the berries are dry.

For new rakes, there is only one company where farmers can go: Hubbard Rakes, located in Jonesport, Maine. Harold Hubbard, known as Ike, proudly assures me he is the only one in the business. He ships to everyone: the world's largest wild blueberry corporations found in Maine, small-scale farmers, and families with backyard berry patches. He has even constructed a 4½-inch version of a blueberry rake for backpackers to take hiking. Ike does not restrict himself to wild blueberries. There are high-bush blueberry rakes, huckleberry rakes, cranberry rakes, and herb rakes. Last year, he sold over eight hundred and sixty rakes, a total of sixty-seven thousand tines. Ike doesn't know when blueberry rakes were first invented, but he suspects it was in the late 1800s and that they were fashioned out of pieces taken from the textile mills. When Ike wants blueberries, he eats warm blueberry pie with a scoop of French vanilla ice cream.

Duncan buys only a few new rakes; most, he unearths in antique shops—forty dollars each. Rake selected and wood box in hand, I trail Duncan toward a low stone wall and a gnarled tree that provides an umbrella of shade. My small patch of shade is an anomaly; many of the boys have stripped off their shirts in the heat. "Start where the berries begin, you don't want any behind you … Wrap your fingers around the handle, but keep your thumb in front." I clutch the wooden handle as if it were the end of a hose—four fingers down, thumb over the top. If it were a hose, water would be splayed into a fan.

Duncan retrieves the rake, now demonstrating the proper movements of raking, breaking down what looks like a fluid motion into stop-action steps. First the rake performs a shallow dive into the foliage, teeth pointed down. Quickly, it levels out to swim horizontally below the surface. It surfaces, foaming with berries, twigs and leaves. Only a foot away from the site of the dive, it rears sharply vertical, the base remaining half submerged. Next comes the tricky part. Duncan jiggles the rake backwards, the bottom of the pan riding the ground, like swans beating white wings along the water in a court dance. The rake's jig is so exuberant that it dislodges berries held between the rods of teeth. If one were to simply wrench the rake from the depths of the bushes, the berries would be mangled by the teeth, gushing juice.

Only after the rake has been properly jiggled can it be lifted out of the bushes completely. The rake pan is a medley of twigs, leaves and fruit; the comb resembles the beginnings of a wicker basket. What looks to be a miniature bush has sprouted between the tines. The boys, Duncan tells me, stand and extract the hangers-on by hand, but that is tedious and unnecessary. Duncan runs his hand along the bottom of the rake, the motion rapid like running a cloth over a table, upside down. Leaves and twigs leap free. With a final flourish, Duncan tips the corner of the rake over the box; its contents tumble out. He turns and passes the rake to me.

Watching closely, eyes squinting, Duncan delivers suggestions. "Lean on your knee then you have a good base." He demonstrates, left leg bent before him. "Don't keep your wrist locked, let it loose ... Keep your thumb in front." I am reminded of an unfortunate dance class in high school where the instructor was forever admonishing me about the arc of my arm or the angle of my inadequately turned out feet. But Duncan does not reprimand; his voice is matter-of-fact. After a few minutes of observation, he leans over to encase my hand in his, large and callused. He guides me in the motion, the rake flying across the bushes, greedily gobbling berries. We reach an area of thick, bulbous clumps. Easy, I assume. Wrong. Duncan details the complication of clumps. They have to be handled gently; sometimes a second hand is even required to hold the teeth and assist in the jiggling. When Duncan rakes, his movements are decisive but tender, his berries dry. He never sweeps an area more than once; there is no need. He tells me his father was the best of rakers, "He never wasted a motion." On a good day, Duncan can fill twenty-three boxes in an hour and a half.

By 10:30, the supply of empty boxes runs low—more can be found back in the barn. I help load crates into the belly of the pickup truck: thirty in all. On the drive down, I ask Duncan if he eats blueberries? The answer: an unequivocal yes. "I love blueberries anyway they come! My weakness is the black variety." At home, Duncan slips berries into numerous dishes: blueberry pie, blueberry cake, blueberry pancakes, blueberries in cereal, blueberries in milk. "Oh hell, there are so many ways to eat blueberries!" But when raking, Duncan never snacks, even to taste a berry or two. "If I did that I wouldn't be able to stop; I would just sit down in the bushes and eat!"

Thickly Wooded

WHAT DAVID BICKFORD is to the twentieth century, the Reverend Daniel Lancaster was to an earlier century. Lancaster's tome, *The History of Gilmanton*, precisely documents Gilmanton facts and figures from 1727 to 1845. Between umber covers are listed in their completeness: town genealogies, land divisions, local printing presses, Academy trustees and the dealings of the Farmers' Mutual Fire Insurance Company. A record of every marriage ceremony was prepared, but was dropped because the history was already too hefty.

Like David, Daniel Lancaster reveled in the details and minutia of memory. He told of a Mr. Morrison, who lost track of the calendar, resulting in an embarrassing neglect of the Sabbath—a mistake that Lancaster assures the reader was never repeated. From Lancaster I learned of Captain Gilman who, while climbing Garrett Hill, broke all his new crockery brought up from Exeter, and of Joseph Badger, who erected the town's first framed building, was the eighteenth family to arrive, and often insisted

upon serving town-wide suppers. Lancaster devoted an entire page to the wanderings of a lost Mrs. Philbrook, alone in the woods in 1765 who, unable to find her way home and terrified of lurking bears and wolves, spent a sleepless night pacing back and forth, back and forth, ululating hymns at the top of her lungs.

Gilmanton is thickly wooded with history. Filling 286 years are arsonists, abandoned mines, and Abenaki tribesmen. There are gnarled stone walls, like graying skeletons beneath a new growth forest of pines. There are the stories of cider mills, syrup shacks, communal creameries, and their remains—sunken logs in the riverbed, a stone foundation in a field. There are rumors of ghosts and accounts of murder.

To a large extent Gilmanton is proud of its history. The Gilmanton Historical Society holds monthly presentations for residents at the former Town Hall in the Iron Works. At the active Town Hall in Four Corners, the Society sells stapled and spiral bound memoirs: *Gilmanton Landmarks*, *A Brief History of Smith Meeting House*, *The Dear Old Lake*, *The Fire Between Fires*.

In the Town Hall's low-ceilinged basement is maintained a two-room museum, open upon request. In the past three years, barely sixty visitors have requested. Under glass are displayed dark wooden spheres from a century-gone bowling alley, leather gloves, the likeness of a two-story house carved into a foot-wide tree fungus, a rusted soap dish and nine flakes of crumbling bog iron—fiery orange—that once tiled the depths of Crystal Lake. Components, wood and iron, of a Hussey plow pattern the floor, along with a corn chopper, spike driver, sap bucket, jig saw, grindstone, bone cutter, barrel header and two charcoal black, unadorned andirons. On the wall hangs a hay knife, hay cutter, buck saw, horseshoes and ox shoes. Next to it all stands a minute wooden bench—brick red, faded, hardly wide enough for a three-year-old, the name "Mudgett" in spindly mustard lettering painted along the back.

The Tree and the Blossom

THE BOOK IS NOT ON THE SHELVES. Scanning my eye along dark wood planks, I find books on John Adams, home baking and the Old Man in the Mountain. None is the book I'm looking for. The Iron Works Library is high-ceilinged, made cavernous by the lack of walls dividing what would otherwise be three sizable rooms. Built in 1916 on the ashes of the Iron Works fire, the building was the first in the region to be constructed with the intention of housing books. The outside is painted white; the inside is robin's-egg-blue and pimply with peeling paint in the corners. The librarian's desk and brick fireplace are central. To the left, multi-colored teddy bears perch atop children's books—no need to search there. To the right, mysteries, histories, biographies, paperback classics, non-fiction—a much more likely location, but still the volume is elusive. M's: Martin, McEwan, McMurtry, Mendelsohn, but then it skips to Michaels. In the L's I find Erik Larson's *Devil in the White City* about Gilmanton's second most notorious native, Herman Mudgett, but that's not who I am looking for now. Neither is it catalogued under "Classics," whose shelves contain Hawthorne, Hemingway, Dickens, Melville, Kipling, and Brontë. The shelf of suggested readings recommends *Angels & Demons, Julie & Julia, To Kill a Mockingbird* and *Playing for Pizza*. It does not suggest the title I am searching for. It seems that the Gilmanton Iron Works Library's book collection lacks a copy of *Peyton Place*.

—⁓—

When Grace Metalious first moved to Gilmanton in 1953, she lived in the middle of the Corners. Before Gilmanton, she had lived in Belmont, Durham, Portsmouth and, for a time, in Texas at an Army base where her husband was stationed. She was born into Manchester mill life and as a child penned stories in her aunt's bathtub. Her mother was a dentist's assistant, her father was a printer and her childhood sweetheart and later husband, George Metalious, was a teacher. Grace was eighteen when she married. At twenty-eight, she moved to Gilmanton with three kids and a surgery that prevented her from having any more children. Feeling despondent, Grace set about conceiving what she termed her "fourth child"—a manuscript typed on the metal rounds of an Underwood.

Grace was the antithesis of a 1950s housewife. She did not chat with the neighbors over the wash and she did not keep house: dirty dishes lay forgotten across the counters. She preferred flannel, blue jeans, sneakers and cigarettes. She drank, at times heavily, and she frequented the Laconia Tavern. Opposed to entertaining, Grace did not stay long in the center of the Corner's life. Gilmanton residents recall her in varying hues, many contradictory. A straighter telling of her life is found in a hefty biography published in 1981 by Emily Toth, a professor at Louisiana State University.

In the fall of 1954, the Metalious family of five deposited thirty-five dollars in rent and moved three miles up from the main road. The hundred-and-fifty-year old house was angled oddly, and topped with a steep roof. It was surrounded by an abundance of flowers, numerous birdhouses and a sign out front that read "It'll Do."

All throughout the winter and into the spring, Grace typed. As the days grew warmer, she kept typing, sending her children outside with lettuce and tomato sandwiches for days in succession. By mid-spring, when her husband was hired as principal of the Gilmanton School, Grace had selected a French-sounding agent from a list in the local library and sent off her manuscript: *The Tree and the Blossom*. In the depths of August, 1955, the Metalious family went swimming one sweltering day and returned home to a telegram: Grace's book had been sold.

Over the next year, Grace travelled back and forth to New York, and her manuscript made even more frequent commutes. Racy scenes were tamed, if only slightly; incest was stricken altogether; and a new, catchier name was assembled. As George accounts in the book he later published about his wife, *The Girl from Peyton Place*, he and Grace fashioned a name from the edges of America, with help from an atlas—Potter Place, New Hampshire, and Payton, Texas. George recalled Grace exclaiming. "Peyton Place. Peyton Place, New Hampshire. Peyton Place,

New England. Peyton Place, USA. Truly a composite of all small towns where ugliness rears its head, and where the people try to hide all the skeletons in their closets."

—⚭—

Esther Scammell, an Iron Works volunteer librarian, was never allowed to read *Peyton Place* growing up. "The Bobbsey Twins was about as far as my mother thought I should read." Esther, petite with wrinkles often stretched in a smile, sits at the desk stamping due dates, wispy orange hair forming a fuzzy halo. Alice Bean, another librarian, is rarely at the librarian's desk; she is most often found reading to a collection of toddlers, pouring apple juice and handing out homemade whoopee pies. She hates having her picture taken and loves to read picture books filled with loud exclamations during story hour. Alice was at college in Vermont when *Peyton Place* was published. She recalls reading it as the book made its clandestine circuit through the women's dorm. Today college students rarely read *Peyton Place* either in their dorms or in their courses. When I read the work a few years ago, I found it tedious. The scandals of the 1950s seem to have since lost their shock value.

Besides the Iron Works Library, there were two other seasonal libraries in Gilmanton; with limited funds, the three libraries each unlocked their doors for roughly seven hours a week. The library in the Corners sits in the center of the village, close to the site of Grace's first Gilmanton residence. It is the two-room building that was once home to the tailor, the hatter, the printer, the cobbler and the judge. Now it houses books. In 1956, Nellie

Clifford, the Corner's librarian refused to added *Peyton Place* to the collection. "This is awful for the town's reputation. I doubt if this library will carry the book. Our annual budget is only one hundred dollars."

The third seasonal library no longer exists. When operating, it was transient in nature. The Lower Gilmanton Library first accumulated in a spare room of a library trustee. When the family was at home the library was open. During the library's lifetime it cycled through five families, occupying front rooms, side rooms, back rooms. It was once aligned along the treads of stairs, and, in old age, it rested in the barn ell of the Kelley's homestead. It was once the only library open—on demand—in the winter. With the library unheated, patrons would scan shelves in overcoats and mittens.

—⁂—

"To a tourist these towns look as peaceful as a postcard picture," Grace told a New York reporter in the summer of 1956. "But if you go beneath that picture, it's like turning over a rock with your foot—all kinds of strange things crawl out. Everybody who lives in town knows what's going on—there are no secrets—but they don't want outsiders to know." A month before *Peyton Place* was published the press came to Gilmanton. The telephone lines were jammed; so too were the roads in the two town centers. Reporters with country road maps came speeding over the hills in search of the real Peyton Place. They came with notebooks and cameras; they stopped residents in the streets and talked their way into living rooms. Up along the ridge in the farmhouse of a close friend, Grace, overwhelmed, hid in a closet.

Within the town borders of Peyton Place, there is only a single mention of a library in 370 pages. The book's heroine, Allison MacKenzie, and her friend, Kathy Ellsworth, spend a hormone-driven winter tucked in a back corner of the local library searching books for the sexiest paragraphs and discussing breasts the color of marble.

As a kid growing up in Gilmanton summers, I too spent time at the library, though with different reading tastes. I used to bike the half mile to the Iron Works Library every Tuesday morning. For years my mom and I would run a summer reading program with Alice and Esther. Passport to Reading, Blast into Reading, Dig into Reading. In the hours spent at the library we would play word games and browse titles.

Just before noon, when the library closed for the day, my brothers Daniel and David and I would take our bikes and position them at the top of Elm Street, which serves as Main Street for Gilmanton Iron Works. In weekly races we pushed off, peddling fast before coasting, our bodies low to the handlebars, over the bridge and the Suncook, past silver maples and blue tinted spruce, up the rise where Elm Street slipped seamlessly into Stage Road, and there we were finally forced to peddle again to crest the next rise.

Grace always denied that Peyton Place was a monoprint of Gilmanton. "It's a composite picture of life in a small New Hampshire town, but it's not Gilmanton." Few believed her, though. The setting and story gave her away.

In Peyton Place, like in Gilmanton, Elm Street substitutes for the traditional Main Street. "I had the idea that the main streets of all small New England towns were named Main Street," remarks the recently arrived school principal and *Peyton Place* stud Tomas Makris. The town's stationmaster replies: "Perhaps ... It is true that the main streets of all *other* small towns are named Main Street. Not, however, in Peyton Place. Here the main street is called Elm Street."

The resemblance is more than map-deep. A major plot line of *Peyton Place* is drawn directly from a Gilmanton scandal. In the book, the stunning sixteen-year-old, Selena Cross, is repeatedly raped by her stepfather Lucas, undergoes an illegal abortion, eventually kills Lucas in self-defense, and buries his body with the help of her younger brother in the sheep pen in the cold of winter. In Grace's original manuscript, Lucas Cross was Selena's biological father, but the publisher deemed incest too vulgar for 1950s sensibilities. Yet, incest was precisely what had taken place in Gilmanton, when, in 1947, the body of Sylvester Roberts was discovered buried in the sheep pen in a farm homestead on Route 140, across from the present-day Tiny Tails Farm. In the real story, Barbara Roberts, a beautiful twenty-year old mill hand, did not stand trial like her literary counterpart. She pleaded guilty and was sentenced to a year in jail. Her younger brother was sentenced to a juvenile institution for his role in the homicide.

—m—

There will soon be another library in the town of Gilmanton. It sits now just short of completion along the main road between the Iron Works and the Corners. At the turn of the twenty-first century, only two out of New Hampshire's 234 cities and towns lacked a year-round library—Gilmanton with a swelling populace of 3,500, and Randolph, with just over 400. There is no conclusive reason for the omission. There have been public libraries in Gilmanton back to the 1890s when the New Hampshire state legislature offered financial support to all bibliophilic towns. But with the Gilmanton residents dispersed to the edges, the villages competed. Three separate libraries persisted, with no one gaining enough favor or tax support to stay open year-round.

A collection of residents with a book club as their hub decided to change the status quo at the turn of the twenty-first century. They set about raising funds and drawing up plans. For their building, they settled not on a white cape or a squat brick construction, but rather a renovated barn. They trudged through barns in Exeter and Epping, clambered into haylofts in Deerfield, Sanbornton, North Hampton and Hooksett. All were dilapidated and water worn. The North Hampton barn, filled with holes in the roof, was better suited for star-gazing. Holes, however, did not detract enough from the otherwise preferred structure. The North Hampton barn was deconstructed, driven seventy miles north and reconstructed in a meadow in 2004. There it sat as money was raised and spent in succession—a roof, then shingles, then a poured concrete floor. Built entirely on donations, the process was halting. Alice and Stan's seven-year old granddaughter gave a dollar. Another family, who could barely afford milk, offered five.

During their first years in Gilmanton, the Metalious family was rarely able to afford their meat, milk or bread. Then one day, less than two months after *Peyton Place* appeared in bookstores, Grace walked into the Gilmanton Corners General Store to settle her tab. In her hand was a personal check from 20th Century Fox made out for the sum of $75,000. The movie would star Lana Turner and eventually gross twenty-five million. Resentment banned Gilmanton as a film site; Camden, Maine, served instead. The book sold 60,000 copies in the first ten days. With the windfall, Grace purchased a used Cadillac, four bathing suits for her daughters and the daughter of her friend, and put a deposit on a long white cape on the border of Gilmanton down near Meadow Pond.

A hundred and fifty years before Grace bought the deed, a Mary Mudgett owned the homestead, the great-great-grandmother of H. H. Holmes. The house still stands today. Ironically, decades after an alcoholic Grace stumbled drunkenly around the house, the property has been transformed by a couple into a vineyard and accompanying winery. Marshall and Sunny Bishop originally moved to Gilmanton from neighboring Gilford with the intention of raising alpacas.

One late July afternoon I drove out to the vineyard at the other edge of town. Marshall and Sunny led me through the sprawling house, pausing in the upstairs bedroom that is reportedly haunted—by Grace, or by an older inhabitant; the reports differ. Our wanderings ended in the winery with an impromptu tasting. Of their seven wines, one is named "Grace"—Marshall's concoction, Seyval and Concord grapes. Perhaps fittingly, the rose-tinted wine starts sweet, but finishes on an astringent note. Though as Sunny notes, she has been told the real Grace preferred vodka. Neither Sunny nor Marshall had read *Peyton Place* before signing the deed to Grace's house. Since then, Sunny has, and both have watched the movie on numerous occasions. "I wouldn't categorize it as literature, but I enjoyed it."

In 1957, *Peyton Place* became one of the most widely read books in America, some claiming its popularity was surpassed only by the Bible. Yet an accurate reader count is difficult. In cities across the country—including Knoxville, Tennessee; Fort Wayne, Indiana; and Boston, Massachusetts—the book was banned. The countries of Canada, Ireland, Australia, and South Africa kept a tight watch for prohibited *Peyton Place* copies within their borders. And in a town in Texas, a drugstore owner sold a copy to a group of teens and was fined.

As Toth recounts, in less than a decade, Grace gained and lost a fortune. She divorced her husband, George, remarried him, and divorced him again. She entertained numerous affairs and developed intense alcoholism. She wrote three more books, *Return to Peyton Place*, *The Tight White Collar* and *No Adam in Eden*, none of which stood without the bulwark of *Peyton Place*, but all of which piggy-backed to the best seller list. She fumed about the distortion of her creation in the hands of Hollywood, and watched in disgust the creation of two blockbuster movies and the development of a primetime TV show. She traveled through Europe, made numerous trips to New York and Hollywood and lived for short periods on Martha's Vineyard. But always she returned to Gilmanton. In spite of threats, cold stares and open hostility from town residents, Grace always considered Gilmanton her safe haven from fame.

And it was Gilmanton, in the end, where Grace would rest. At the age of thirty-nine, Grace was admitted in February 1964 to Beth Israel Hospital in Boston. Three days later she died, a victim of cirrhosis and a decade of alcoholism. In a will she revised the day before she died, she bequeathed her body to Dartmouth Medical School and her estate to her current lover. Neither wish would be granted. Her family would contest the will and the medical school, not wishing to get involved in legal wrangling, would decline the body. In the winter of 1964, Grace's body returned once more to Gilmanton—all except her eyes, which were successfully donated to a Boston eye bank. Throughout a particularly snowy winter, Grace's body lay in a crypt waiting for spring and the ground to thaw. Despite indignation by certain residents of the town, Grace was buried in Smith Meeting House—a minor funeral with only twenty-five in attendance.

University scholars have touted Metalious as a force for social change, a feminist army of one, a woman misunderstood and mistreated. Others take a stoutly opposing stance, discrediting her skill and decrying her as slanderous. In Gilmanton these two camps carve out equal territory. Portraits of Grace come only in black or only in white. Half a century appears still too short a time to understand the writer in subtler shades.

—◆◆◆—

I return to the Iron Works Library to make one final sweep of the shelves. Spotting an ochre card catalogue off in a corner,

I investigate. There it is: "Metalious, Grace. Peyton Place" in red cursive. Card in hand, I find Alice. She leads me not to a shelf, but to her librarian's desk. The bottom drawer jams just a little before opening. Inside, amongst papers and pencil stubs, is a black book with a fraying spine and silver lettering spelling *Peyton Place.* "If I put it out on the shelves," Alice explains. "I'm afraid it might be stolen and burned. I'm not saying that's what would necessarily happen, but you just don't know."

Come As You Are

In the predawn of May 28, 1915, a Friday, Mr. Osborn Price awakened to the smell of smoke. On investigation, he discovered a shattered window and a waltzing blaze consuming his shed along Elm Street in the center of the Iron Works. The fire was modest, and with the assistance of two buckets, he doused it dead and returned to bed. An hour later, he woke again to the smell of smoke. A quick check confirmed that his shed was safe, but he saw, on a neighboring property, a barn painted flickering gold. Within four hours, downtown Gilmanton Iron Works would turn charcoal black, charred timbers drawing only the sketch of a town.

While both, I believe, would have reveled in the telling, neither Daniel Lancaster nor David Bickford can provide history with a blow-by-blow of that early morning in May. If they could, I am certain we would know which volunteers stood in a line passing buckets hand-to-hand in futility. We would picture in vivid detail mothers, daughters, grandmothers racing from their homes, dressing gowns flapping, family mementos clutched to their bosoms. We would be certain of the man navigating the horse-drawn Paugus pumper, hand-operated, from Alton—perfunctory without an easily accessible water source and no fire department in Gilmanton. We would undoubtedly be sure as to which forty danced close to the blaze with the totality of the town's fire extinguishers clasped between their sweaty palms. Though no resident lost his life that morning, the tally of cows, sheep, goats, and chickens consumed in the conflagration, I am confident, would have been dutifully recorded. The sound of ten pounds of dynamite splintering the corner store, set off in a vain attempt to foil the flames, would reverberate in our ears. We would know, with no need for imagination, which buildings were the first to fall, collapsing inwards, great fireworks of debris thrown up into the air, and how the stained glass oozed like maple syrup down the white walls of the church. Unfortunately, on the morning of May 28, Lancaster was dead over thirty years and David was all of two years old and, as he notes, "I wasn't yet a member of the fire department."

—⁂—

By the time he retired in 1962, David would serve twenty-eight years on the volunteer firemen's roster, including two as chief. Over nearly three decades, he would sample every office in the Gilmanton fire department. As entertainment chair, David organized oyster suppers, lobster bakes and masquerade balls (at 25 cents and 50 cents a ticket) to raise money to purchase portable pumps and a thousand feet of hose. The town allotted only three hundred dollars a year to the fire department. Fire department parties were ignited with such regularity that they soon became relied on for weekly entertainment. The firemen themselves went unpaid till the 1980s. Extinguishing forest fires, a task partially supervised by the state, did pay. David pocketed fifty cents an hour for every forest fire he helped douse. The department navigated low-riding Chevrolet engines, paid for, in part with Lizzy's pies. David often drove. The firemen mixed cocktails of soda, acid and water and served them to the tanks (two forty-gallon jobs) to build pressure.

Fires called in by town folk set red phones ringing in three houses. David answered one. It sat in his entryway, "away from my other phone." When the red phone rang, he took off to the firehouse—white with rufous garage doors—and now up for sale. There were no uniforms: fires were come-as-you-are affairs. David's head and arms are spotted and scabbed from burns from a garage fire in the forties, which he quenched wearing only pants and a T-shirt as protection. Another time, fighting a fire at John Page's house, "This was in cold weather, down below zero ... The house was on fire from the inside in the kitchen and it had spread to the upper floor. They had asbestos shingles so it wasn't burning on the outside. I was up on a ladder and had a hose going through the window, working on that upper part, and the others were of course working on that lower part. We didn't have helmets, raincoats, anything. I just had on an ordinary coat. So here I am working that window from upstairs and someone comes over from the other side and they put a string of water up through the window and it caught me and it just soaked my outer clothes. They froze practically as quick as it hit."

Despite the parties, and extra pumps and engines that they funded, the fire department all too often had a negligible effect on any sizable conflagration. The men were simply too ill-equipped; like gnats around a black bear, the firemen were, to the flames, an annoyance only. David shakes his head, "Well, we saved a lot of chimneys." Fires frequently blossomed in chimney stalks, igniting creosote build-up and from there spinning fire webs outward through the house; filthy chimney linings fed flames—an ultimate reprimand for neglected chores. Certain homes were particularly negligent; David remembers two—one on Halls Hill and another right in the center of the Iron Works. The firemen took preventive measures—they added chimney sweep to their resumes–finding it simpler to clean the flues than deal with the fiery consequences.

David once smoked out a suspected arsonist, trailing him across the hills of Gilmanton. "We would have mysterious fires and this particular man was always in the area." The man in question, a fireman himself, once raised the alarm for a fire up on Alton Road. The men arrived to find themselves made redundant by two couples up from the city that had noticed the blaze on their excursion to the movies and promptly smothered the last of the flames with sand. They reported passing a black pickup bouncing boisterously down the road to town. The suspected fireman drove the same. On another occasion, the fireman directed the department deep into the woods in pursuit of a brush fire so small that the lugged back-pumps proved superfluous. There was a third fire at a barn on Route 140, across from what is now Tiny Tails Farm. If the fires were indeed set by the rogue fireman, three seems to have been his lucky number. The fire caught and the barn burned to high heaven.

—m—

Extracted from the rubble and ash of the Great Iron Works Fire of 1915 were, among other items, an empty kerosene can—buried in the debris at the site of the fire's genesis. The evidence suggested arson. There would be those who waggled fingers at a Jennie Keys, others at a Marion Tuttle. Both were cantankerous and both lost homes to the flames. Gilmanton announced a three-hundred-dollar reward, but it remained uncollected. *The Boston Daily Globe* published a column-long article implicating Mrs. Tuttle, but ruefully retracted it twenty-one days later on learning Mrs. Tuttle had slept peacefully through the fire in a bed eighteen miles away. The fine silver possessed by Mrs. Keys required only a thorough scrub once the embers were extinguished, as every piece had been deposited in the mud of the Suncook at some undetermined time before the blaze. Mrs. Keys would die, never formally accused, in a state asylum.

—m—

David's firefighting career ended on a Sunday. The account involved a church, sending up smoke instead of prayers. "I was down with my brother, Clarence, and his son, Richard, ice fishing on Suncook Pond. And the doggone siren started blowing. So I started running up the hill and here I am around about fifty. Richard of course was lots younger and carrying a little more weight. I was gaining on him and I got right to the top of the hill coming up from the pond to Clarence's house and it was just like they put a band around me tight and I pretty much hit the ground." David suffered a hiatal hernia, and then a heart condition. His cardiologist banned fire fighting from his weekly routine.

The fire siren that once reverberated across the Gilmanton hills still stands sentinel—an erect toadstool on the roof of a partially abandoned building that is Old Town Hall, once New Town Hall, and before that Odd Fellows Hall. In a century, its auditorium has held selectmen's offices, town-wide meetings, weddings, graduation ceremonies, Crystal Lake Grange councils on the second floor, and Highland Lodge conclaves on the first. In the basement, elementary school classes were once conducted; today, the dealings of the town's police. Below pressed tin tiles, sepia in hue, the town's youth once cavorted on floors

glossy with paste wax and elbow grease. On Saturdays, they might dance a two-step, quadrille, waltz, duchess, galop, or the concentric circles of a Portland Fancy. On special occasions perhaps a square dance or a barn dance ("wear overalls, aprons or gingham gowns"), with the added excitement of nail-driving, milk-drinking, and doughnut-eating contests.

Today the high-ceilinged halls are locked, the once polished floor dusty with bat guano and desiccated flies. Written permission from a town selectman is required to ascend four staircases and a wooden ladder to the four-windowed tower room below the siren. The abandoned halls now host graffitied school desks, town reports, and World War II infirmary cots, stacked and folded. In benches, fifty-year-old student plays and wallpaper catalogues in mauve, beige and mustard deteriorate. In a corner slouches a wooden barrel for kindling, girdled not with iron but birch.

Years have slipped away since the hills reverberated with the siren's regular squawk. Occasionally, it is tripped accidentally. Four months ago was one such occurrence and police chief can attest, "It is loud!" When still in operation, two bellows from the siren warned of flames between Price's farm and Smith Meeting House, six for between Bickford's Corner and Lower Gilmanton. One long deep blast at precisely 7:45 a.m. heralded no school for the day.

A hundred years ago, if I were to stand in Odd Fellows tower, Gilmanton spilling out below me in ripples, I would hardly recognize the town. For one thing, I would see farther—farms still operating, forest still kept at bay. Mill Road would not yet be overgrown and the Suncook River would scribble its way through the fields, a thick line of ballpoint ink on green. There would be no big rusted red siren. It would not be installed until 1929. But most striking would be the Iron Works itself. A hundred years ago, there were three stores not one—Chase's Store, C.A. Dockham's Store and Mitchell & Cutcliff. A hundred years back, there stood a tannery, a hotel, a school, a mill and a Free Will Baptist church. All turned to ash in May 1915, along with a post office, a library, thirteen homes, a line of elm and maple trees fringing the road, the village's only clock—presented to the church by a man up from New York City—and all the town records. The total destruction would be estimated at seventy thousand dollars, and would include the entirety of the Iron Works business establishment save a single shop. Odd Fellows Hall escaped fiery consumption by only a few feet.

August

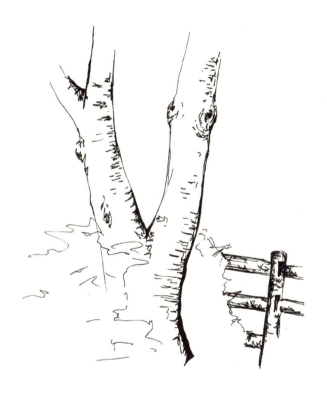

August in Gilmanton is when the crops come in en masse. Knobbly carrots are uprooted in handfuls; onions too. If July rains have been lenient and fleshy verdant hornworms scarce, tomatoes—beef, cherry, zebra-striped—are plentiful. The first sweet corn is shucked. Zucchinis are watched religiously—if not, they transform overnight from frankfurters to major-league baseball bats. Zucchinis are so numerous in August that they are given away by the bagful, sometimes surreptitiously deposited on doorsteps to prevent recipients from refusing. In August our small vegetable garden is overrun with baseball bats. We eat stuffed zucchini, grilled zucchini, thinly shaved raw zucchini salad drizzled in lemon and oil. I stir up batch after batch of extra-moist zucchini bread with double- and triple-squash proportions.

Farm stands across Gilmanton explode in color. The first of Tiny Tail's peaches are arranged in baskets for sale. Peaked Hill Farm near the Corners puts out tubs of squash, broccoli, fingerling potatoes. Road stalls are unmanned, with honesty boxes. On Wednesday afternoons, farms across the town truck squash, corn, beans, home baked breads and cured lamb sausages, and set up tables across the green in front of Town Hall. Our meals become effortlessly local.

Come August my brothers and I take our sleeping bags outside. We lay them at odd angles on the grass under clear, star filled skies. July is firmly planted in summer—wet and carefree. August is hot and parched, but at night it turns cold.

The stars of Gilmanton are nothing like city stars. The sky is Van Gogh, it is Seurat, it is Sargent—translucent light on pitch. The Milky Way is painted in shimmering brush strokes, banding the sky. By mid-August, the Pleiades send monsoons of fireballs down upon us.

Out on the night grass, slightly damp, pines and birch are the only silhouettes. There are no houselights, streetlights, flashing store signs to blur the view. Only an occasional car's headlights sweep across our vision. Because of the chill, mosquitoes go into hiding. An occasional raccoon creeps its way to the birdfeeder. Some nights the neighbor's coydogs howl. The howls echo.

Often I fall asleep on the grass, eyes trained on the stars. Leaving would be a form of resignation, staying a means of holding back time. The night sky is limitless and, by association, so too summer.

By the Shape of Their Hooves

WHEN CHARLES, CHUCK AS HE PREFERS, was ten he used to help his father by feeding the newborn calves. By the time he was fifteen he was helping milk the 1,500-pound, full-grown Holsteins most evenings after school. When Chuck graduated high school, he started working full time on the farm. Forty-five years later, now with a balding crown and a clean-shaven rugged face, Chuck grins, "I never thought of doing anything else; I always enjoyed working with my father." Chuck works alongside his own son now. Recently he has been teaching his fourteen-year-old grandson, Caleb, how to work with cows.

The Price Family farm spreads over four hundred acres across both sides of Shannon Road and spills onto the far side of Route 140. The farm is six-generations old—one of the oldest remaining farms in Gilmanton. Four generations help on the farm today. Chuck and his 39-year-old son, Jon, do the majority of the farm work, but Caleb is beginning to help with the milking. Pauline, Chuck's mother, is still spry at eighty-eight, keeping

the house and the barn meticulously clean. "She doesn't stop," Jon chuckles. "It would drive her nuts to just sit up in the house."

Our family has frequented the Price Farm for as long as I can remember. We drive the half-mile up the road for maple syrup. In the spring when sap courses through the sugar maples, the Prices stoke the stoves in the sugar shack and set the liquid to boil. I like to stand in the shack, close my eyes and inhale the steam.

But the shack is closed and locked now and the year's syrup bottled, labeled, shelved, and ready to sell. This time I'm not coming for syrup, but to learn about cows.

—⁊⁊—

By five p.m., four of us are in the parlor. This is no nineteenth-century Victorian parlor ornamented with heavy draperies, satin wrapped chairs and fragile tea sets. On Price Farm it is a milking parlor, and it caters to cows. The room is divided into thirds, with the middle section sunk low and carpeted in black rubber matting. It is from this vantage point that we four—three generations of Price men and myself—are given a full-on view of ten bovine butts.

The Price Farm is home to Holstein cows. They are the canonical cow of postcards, a boxy breed splattered in black and white paint. They are prized for their dairy production and on occasion for their appearance. In the early twentieth century President Taft kept a Holstein as a pet who roamed the White House lawns and produced quality milk for the First Family.

The cows come in in groups of five and line up, with only minimal prompting, in angled corrals along two corridors flanking the sunken center aisle. They stand benignly as the three men move back and forth preparing each for milking. Chuck and Jon are in the parlor every day, twice a day. Still in school, Caleb helps at least two afternoons a week. The Prices are used to the routine and each other; their movements are dance-like and coordinated.

Chuck narrates the process as he takes a bristle brush from a cabinet. "First thing you have to do is brush off the udder. The cows bed down in sand and you need to make sure the udders are completely clean before milking." He gives the udders of his cow a quick scrub. He exchanges the brush for a green plastic cup filled with a molasses colored liquid and dips each teat in it like a chocolatier might dip fruit. "Iodine," Chuck explains. "We use it before we milk and right after to help prevent infection." The Prices are always on the look out for mastitis, a bacterial disease that can affect the composition of the milk, turning it off color or lumpy. From an overhead dispenser, Chuck snags a paper towel and wipes down the teat. Before attaching the milker he checks each teat by hand, gripping it firmly at the top and squeezing out three long streams of steaming milk. "Most of the bacteria collects in the bottom of the udder and we don't want that getting into the milk." The hand milking also allows Chuck to spot infection—discoloration or clotting. With the cow's udders thoroughly cleaned, it is time for milking.

The milking machine resembles a mechanical squid with four narrow cups that suction to each udder. The cups connect through black tubing to a central "claw" that funnels the milk through a large clear tube, sending the milk streaming into glass eggs three feet tall that hold just over 65 pounds of milk. In the stores, milk is measured in gallons, but here on the farm it is recorded in pounds.

Chuck beckons me over. He is holding out one of the vacuum cups and tells me to stick my finger in. He flips a switch and the vacuum kicks in, the squid attempts to milk my index finger, squeezing and pulsating, mimicking the action of hand milking.

I retrieve my finger and Chuck holds the machine up in front of me. "Hold the claw in your left hand so it's horizontal," he demonstrates before passing it over to me. "Now take a cup and bring it up, but kink the tube as you do it. Otherwise the vacuum will shoot air up into the teat and bacteria can get in and cause infection."

With this warning he hands me the claw. It takes me two tries, the first time the tube unkinks early and the vacuum attempts to suction my cow's hind leg. I get a better grip on the cup and angle my torso so I'm leaning closer to the udders, hoping the cow won't kick. Positioning the cup directly under an udder I un-kink the tube and the cup shoots upward over the teat. Success. Three more to go.

When the Price men hook up a cow to the milker, the motion is fluid, rapid, and takes less than a minute. With ten cows milking at once it sounds as if we are standing within a gigantic washing machine.

—ɯ—

Chuck is named for his great-great-grandfather Charles Amos Price whose family came from Manchester, N.H., and who was gifted the 430-acre farm as a wedding present in 1845. There were fewer cows on the farm a century and a half ago and those that they had were primarily beef breeds. Charles's son was Amos Richard Price who went by Amos. His son was also Amos Richard Price, but he went by Richard. Richard, Chuck's father, was the first Price to switch the farm's focus from beef to dairy. He started with six cows and milked each by hand.

—ɯ—

I was told to arrive at three p.m. just in time for the second milking of the day. I find Chuck and Jon out in the back with the right front wheel of their tractor on the ground and a worn roller bearing clasped tight in a clamp. Jon has been noticing a slight wobble in the wheel and they've taken the time between the two milkings today to assess the damage.

While my day on the farm is starting in the late afternoon Chuck and Jon's day began at ten to five this morning. Before meeting his father in the barn, Jon always puts on a large pot of coffee. They clean out the stalls, set the first ten cows to milk and Jon goes back up to the house to fill up their mugs. Both father and son drink their coffee with liberal amounts of raw milk and cream. "I have to have cream in it," laughs Chuck. I ask if he ever drinks his coffee black. "I have to support the dairy farmers."

The Price men only drink raw milk. "I think it has more taste," Chuck considers. "It's got more flavor. I think heating it up takes away from the milk. This is what I was brought up on." He screws up his face as he says it. "One percent tastes like water. I like something I can chew on." Chew on?

How much milk does Chuck drink? He laughs again, a deep rumbling laugh that rolls over itself. "Seems like I'm always getting milk." He and his wife drink up to two gallons a week. "But I've cut back a lot. I used to sit down and have four or five glasses of milk in one sitting. Now I have just two glasses a day, one at lunch and one at supper. I'm trying to cut back." He pats his belly—a belly which barely protrudes past his belt line.

The milking is finished by 8:30 and the top priority is breakfast before a day of fieldwork. Chuck and Jon consume large bowls of cereal (with milk) and OJ.

In the winter Chuck might sip a cup of cocoa with his cereal. He admits slyly, "So I get a little more milk then."

By 3:30, after a day that can include everything from tractor repairs, to seeding or haying fields, to boiling and bottling maple syrup—depending on the season—it is time for the day's second milking.

Looking at his watch Chuck nods, "About time to start." He turns to me. "Follow me over here. You are going to need boots." We traipse into the barn where a line of black rubber boots stand ready. Unlacing my sneakers I slip my feet into a pair that envelop my legs to just below my knees. Properly attired I follow Chuck out into the back barn. "The first thing we got to do is clean out the stalls of the young heifers."

The barn, Chuck tells me, used to hold sheep. "But I don't remember the sheep. Years ago they used to have sheep everywhere, all over New Hampshire. That used to be the thing, sheep, sheep, sheep." Now there are cows—six heifers that are six to seven months old and eight heifers that are five months and younger.

Chuck takes down a rake with a long horizontal blade of metal like an ice scraper, and begins pushing manure out of the barn. "Come on girls, come on. You've got to move a little." Chuck coos to the cows. They shuffle along with Chuck bringing up the rear pushing manure. Two heifers sidle over to investigate me. "Come on girls. What? You like her? Oh you're trying to lick her, huh?" They stick their heads between the wooden beams of the stall and stretch out their tongues to taste the strap of my bag. "They love to lick!"

Cows grow quickly. By the time the heifers are two years old they weigh 1,200 pounds and they will be ready to calve. "We try to grow them quick. The quicker you can get them into milk the quicker you can start getting money back." As the baby cows continue to snuffle at my clothing, Chuck finishes scraping out the last of the manure. Out in the main barn where the milking herd is, Jon will do the same. "A major part of the dairy business is manure," Jon concedes. Protected by their tall rubber boots, the men clean the barns three times a day, once before and once after the morning milking and once again after the second milking. They collect the manure in a holding pond and every couple of weeks fill a spreader and drive out to enrich their fields with feces. The manure makes gloopy sloshing noises as the men sweep at it with their metal brooms. "We feed them a pretty rich diet. That's why their manure is really loose," Chuck explains.

Out behind the barn runs a long concrete trough. Twice a day the Prices fill its length with haylage, a minced mix of chopped corn, hay and grain. Leaning over I pick up a handful of the moist grasses and rub it between my fingers. Haylage is fermented slightly and smells sweet like molasses. One cow will eat upwards of seventy pounds of haylage a day. "They can put away a lot of fuel," laughs Chuck. For the entire herd the Prices lay out a spread of 2,500 pounds of grass and 800 pounds of grain—a ton and a half of food in total.

Years ago the Prices used to feed the cows grain in the milk parlor. "Back then they would be lining up to come in for milking." Now because the grain is mixed into the haylage for a more balanced diet, Chuck must herd the cows into the parlor, but he needs no sticks or dogs, just a calm coaxing voice. "OK, girls let's go. Let's get up. Come on girls. Up you get." Some of the cows are resting in the stalls and they take their time getting up, like a person pushing a snooze button repeatedly. As they plod out of the barn, a holdup ensues as they catch sight of me. As with the baby heifers, the cows are curious and form a line of large boxy

heads. They stare at me, large black eyes taking me in. Their muzzles jut forward to sniff at the air around me. A few of the less trepidatious take small steps forward and stretch out their long purple tongues to lick my outstretched palm.

— m —

A good milking cow might produce upward of a hundred pounds of milk in a day, approximately ten gallons or more. A consistently producing Price cow will milk three hundred days a year, with fifty vacation days before birthing. As they grow older a heifer's milk production tapers, but if they reside on the farm for the typical ten years they might produce a total of 30,000 gallons of milk. The farm's annual milk production in supermarket quart cartons standing side-by-side would stretch forty miles, roughly the distance from the Price Farm to the state capital of Concord and back. In the parlor a cow's daily milking takes only eight minutes.

Every other morning the company Agri-Mark drives to the Price Farm to pick up milk. This morning the truck came and left before my arrival, taking with it 8,600 pounds of pasteurized milk. The milk sloshes its way to factories owned by the Cabot Creamery Cooperative. There the Price Farm milk will be stirred with the milks of half the family farms in New England; Cabot is a co-op of more than two thousand small farms. After processing, Price Farm milk might emerge on supermarket shelves as milk—sometimes even one percent, notwithstanding Chuck's disdain—or, as heavy sweet cream, condensed milk, yogurt, butter, cottage cheese, or cheddar cheese.

A loud sucking noise brings our attention to the third cow on the right. She's managed to kick off the milking machine, and the vacuum cups are lying jumbled at her feet, gasping like fish out of water. Chuck turns to untangle the claw from a cow's feet who is known to be something of a kicker. Smiling, Jon looks over while setting up another cow. "Chuck, you stopped baby-sitting."

Like his father, farm life is the only life Jon has ever known. "It's the only job I've ever had, full time." Right out of high school, Jon contemplated joining the Army. "But I knew that I had this farm and if I went off who would help my dad?" From the time he was younger than his own son, Caleb, Jon can remember helping on the farm. "I used to follow my dad around the farm doing what I could. I was happy just to ride around with him on the tractor. I loved it."

For Jon, the joy of farming is in the variety. "I love the whole operation, but particularly the change from one project to the next." Like farms across America, chores are dictated by the seasons. April and May are for planting—the vegetable garden and the thirty acres of cornfields. June is for harvesting the first crop of hay. Ample rain in July brings the Prices out again in August to cut a second crop. They store the hay in a silo skirting the forest and weighted under tires. "In the fall we get a little break … Well I say we get a little break, there is always equipment to repair and other things around the farm, and there are always the cows."

When the ground freezes and snow begins to fall, it is time to log wood: 15,000 board feet of lumber, sixty cords of firewood. The Prices don't sell the wood they cut, but use the firewood themselves, in the large furnace behind the barn that sends pipes snaking into the house and the parlor. Come April, wood burns across the road to heat sap in the two-room maple sugar shack.

Maple syrup season is Caleb's favorite time of year. He, like me, loves the sweet steam of the sugar as the sap traverses back

and forth through the canals of the boiler, transforming from semi-sweet water to a viscous amber syrup.

In mid-March the Prices take miles of clear tubing and walk out into their woods to tap sugar maples. "People have been tapping maple trees around here as far back as I can remember, probably as long as farms have been running," Chuck muses. Traditionally, trees are tapped with three-inch spiles hammered into tree veins that channel the sap into metal buckets. In recent years tubing has replaced buckets on farms that boil syrup en masse; it is a more efficient system. "But we keep about fifty buckets up along the road," Chuck explains. "They are mostly for show. They look nice." Sap flows best when the days are warm and the nights are cold. In a good year the syrup season lasts four to six weeks. During that time the Prices might siphon 7,000 gallons of sap. After hours and hours of boiling that sap will reduce down to 200 gallons of concentrated syrup.

Caleb eats syrup on his waffles and his pancakes and even on his ice cream. Chuck pours syrup over his cereal every morning. "I use the darkest grade of syrup I can get." In the barn there is a triangular closet that contains a treasure trove of liquid amber. The bottles of syrup are taupe-tinted plastic and resemble old-fashioned jugs with tiny finger handles near the lids. The closet holds shelves of half pints, pints, quarts, half gallons and sinfully large gallon jugs that I have yet to commit to buying.

Customers come from all over to buy the Price's maple syrup. There is no website for sales, just a wood sign out near the road. There are the regular customers and then there are the visitors who drive by, see the sign and stop. "There was a couple here yesterday from Australia. They bought eight half pints to take back with them." Visitors who stop once often call up a year later asking for more. Chuck ships syrup across the country to homes as far as Utah and Oregon. For twenty years he shipped a one-gallon jug to an elderly lady in Switzerland. "The cost of shipping was about the same as the cost of the syrup, but she had to have her syrup."

In early spring, during syrup season the ground and trees are blanketed in snow. Even the cows become covered. Cows love the cold, much more than they do the heat of summer. With insulated coats, the snow doesn't melt off their backs. Instead it accumulates, rising higher and higher.

—∞—

Along the left line of cows, Chuck is decorating a back leg with a yellow Velcro anklet. This particular cow is pregnant and just a couple months from term. The yellow band reminds the Prices that she is drying off. They'll milk her once a day in the mornings for a week and then she'll be on holiday for approximately fifty days before she gives birth. "We give them a dry spell before they calf as a respite," Chuck explains, fastening the band securely around her leg. "They get a fifty-day vacation. How would you like to have one of those?!"

A green band around an ankle designates a three-teeter cow—a heifer that might have an infection in one udder. A red band is for infection—that cow's milk won't go in with the rest. A red band can also be used to identify a cow that has just given birth.

"You should have been here last night," Chuck tells me. "We

had a cow give birth around 6:30." Because this is a working dairy farm, a cow will stay with its newborn baby for only a few hours, enough time to lick it clean, but not enough for either to form an attachment with each other. It becomes harder on everyone otherwise, so the mother rejoins the herd and the baby joins a mini-herd of other babies and is hand fed from a bottle. Chuck points out the new mother along the line of milkers to the left.

Jon is hooking her up for milking, but before turning on the machine he flips a switch diverting the milk from the glass egg and into a metal bucket on the floor. "You don't want to drink this milk," he explains. "It's just got a lot of goodies in it and we save that for the calves." A mother's milk right after birthing is called colostrum and is teeming with antibodies and vitamins needed to help a newborn cow navigate on wobbly legs. The milk that streams out into the bucket is thick, yellow, and resembles pancake batter. Jon has never tasted it, "It feels thicker, almost slimy." "You mean slippery," Chuck interjects. "Yeah, slippery sounds better."

"Want to come with me?" Caleb calls from the stair. Thin with straw blond hair, Caleb has changed from school clothes into basketball shorts and a gray T-shirt. "I'm going to go feed the newborn." I follow him out of the parlor, past the barn where the milked cows are congregating and out to the shed where the smallest calves stay. A healthy newborn comes into the world weighing a hundred pounds.

Peering in at the curled-up calf, it is hard to believe she is less than twenty-four hours old. "They are still wobbly on their feet and they don't know how to nurse well yet so you have to help them," Caleb explains. He passes me a baby bottle the size of my forearm with a long pink nipple. Under Caleb's instructions I stick my finger in the calf's mouth; its tongue wraps inquisitively around my index finger and suckles. Only then do I exchange my finger for the bottle's nipple. The calf still doesn't have the process down perfect and by the time she has successfully consumed a bottle's worth of milk my hand is dripping with cow drool and milk. "She'll get the hang of it in a couple of days and then we switch her to drinking from a bowl." From a bowl a calf can easily slurp up four pints of frothy milk in thirty seconds.

Caleb is the sixth generation of Price farmers, but he's undecided yet whether he will stay on the farm. "I want to, but I'm also a science fanatic. I love chemical engineering. But I would also like to keep the farm running." Could he combine the two? "We've talked about that. We artificially inseminate all our cows and that has a lot to do with genetics, so maybe I can." Talking about inseminating cows would send most fourteen-year-old boys snickering, but for Caleb it is just another part of farm life.

Back in the parlor, Chuck explains that when his parents ran the farm the cows produced thirty pounds of milk a day. Today the Price's cows produce on average seventy pounds per day. What has changed? "Mostly the genetics."

There are no full-grown bulls on the farm. Instead, every few months Chuck and Jon sit down with a catalogue of hundreds of bulls and shop for traits. They pick their bulls for a variety of desirable traits: better feet, better udders. "For example, if you have a cow with a sloppy udder you can pick a fuller-udder bull and you have a lot better chance of having a calf with a better

udder." When it is time to impregnate a cow, a company called
GENEX drives out to the farm with a truck full of sperm. No ice
cream truck ditties here. Chuck buys sperm at twelve to fifteen
dollars a pop. He passes on what he terms "super semen," prize
bull sperm that trades for Ben Franklins. "That's for people who
are into showing and selling."

Nine months after a visit from the sperm truck a new calf will
hopefully be born. Approximately eighty calves are born on the
farm every year. Almost half are bulls and are sold almost imme-
diately to an auction house down in Massachusetts. A hundred
bucks per bull. Of the heifers, the Prices will keep fifteen of the
most promising. They will grow up on the farm and join the herd.

In all the years that Chuck has lived and worked on the farm,
almost half a century, he has never once bought a cow. He sells
cows—when they get too old, or if they become lame. But his
entire herd has been born and raised on the farm. The sixth generation of Prices is now tending the thirtieth generation of cows.

Currently, there are sixty-five milkers on the farm. Jon and
Chuck know each personally. Where I see a blanket of black and
white patterning, the Prices see a herd of individuals. Each cow
has ear tags and numbers, but they seem superfluous to the farmers. "Over there at the end," Jon points to a cow at the end of the
milking line. "That's number 99. She is our oldest milking cow
right now, almost eleven years old." How do you know for sure
that's her, I press. "She's been here for ten years, I just recognize
her. Certain cows I can tell. Like I know that is 147 and that's
number 19. I can tell by the shape of her udder, her colors, I know
she has a lot of white on her." Chuck can tell his cows apart simply

by looking at their feet. Jon laughs, "I'm out here all the time. I do a pretty good job recognizing the cows, better than remembering someone's name." The cows by tradition are not christened with names, just numbers. "I mean a couple we have a name for," Jon admits. "But we won't mention what they are." He rolls his eyes, shaking his head at the cows. But recently Jon's wife has decided to single one out from the herd. Jon points her out to me, a young heifer with long glossy black and white variegated hair hanging down between her ears. "My wife calls her Bangs."

—⁂—

By 6:30 even the stragglers have been milked. The barns have been cleaned, the cows fed and all that is left is to clean the parlor and set the milking equipment to wash. All the equipment undergoes three thorough wash cycles after every milking. As the men are finishing up, Chuck's wife, Marie, pokes her head into the parlor, an old Tropicana jug in her hand—they have run out of milk in the house and need to get more.

Chuck collects his raw milk from the 1,600-gallon stainless steel tank that sits in the milk room. A ladder scales the side of the tank. "Climb up." Opening the hatch I'm looking down on a churning sea of milk. "Want to take a milk bath?" Chuck calls up. From a nozzle at the bottom of the tank, Chuck siphons milk for the family. Crouching down he holds a metal pitcher to the spout. "This is how the farmer gets his milk." He transfers the milk into the old plastic carton. Then with a grin, downs the few sips left in the pitcher. "I always overfill it a little so I can drink the extra. It's still warm."

With chores complete we head out of the barn. I slip my feet out of the rubber boots and lace up my sneakers. Caleb and Jon head inside the house. Caleb still has homework to complete. Chuck follows me outside to where his own car is. His house is half a mile up the road and his plans for the evening are dinner and then bed. What will he have to eat? "I don't know!" He laughs and then adds, "But I do know I'll have a tall glass of milk."

In Black and White

In the pages of the *Laconia Democrat* and the *News & Critic*, national history was played out on a small scale. In the early years of the 1900s, local temperance movements turned town taps off, on, off, on until Prohibition, although home-brewed cider remained accessible throughout. Automobiles started puttering the back roads of Gilmanton by the turn of the century. Every purchase and each afternoon drive was proudly proclaimed in newsprint: a brand new REO Speed wagon, a Studebaker Auto. But while the leisurely drives of an Elwin Edgerly might have been newsworthy in the 1920s, by the 1930s it was the sight of horses employed for mail delivery that was a source of astonishment when mud made the roads nearly impassable for automobiles.

In the Corners, the Academy's bell rang from sun-up to sundown, punctuated by cannon blasts, on November 11, 1918. Sandwiches, doughnuts, and coffee were abundant. A bonfire blazed on the lawn, and a likeness of Kaiser Wilhelm the Second, last emperor of Germany, was burned to nothingness. A year later the first plane was spotted at four p.m. on a Thursday as it navigated from the Weirs, a town just west, to Boston at 2,500 feet. The twenties were brighter as Gilmanton homes installed electricity. But the center streets of the Iron Works would not be lamp-lit until 1928. The lamps have since been dismantled. By 1931 the sole surviving Gilmanton soldier of the Civil War would celebrate his eighty-ninth birthday, the last of 149 who enlisted.

Reading the newspaper, one could keep abreast of who was off visiting sisters in Boston or cousins in Somersworth, who had a slight cold and what unfortunate soul had cleaved his foot while chopping cordwood. In black, white and gray, the local papers painted Gilmanton.

City boarders and potato bugs are quite plentiful in this part of the town. (*News and Critic*, July 24, 1896)

One of the Gilmanton farmers who recently lost a favorite cow, concluded [the cow's] eulogy by remarking that she was as handsome as a school marm. This was praise enough for the cow but rather tough on the school marms. (*Laconia Democrat*, February 22, 1895)

The Rhode Island Red hen of Mrs. Minnie Moham of Hackett Hill must surrender the belt to one owned by our correspondent which last week laid a two-yolk egg that measured 6 ½ x 8 ½ inches and made a fine omelet for two of us. (*News and Critic*, April 23, 1919)

Bushels begat bragging rights: twenty-five bushels of cherries, 150 bushels of strawberries. In the summer of 1889 a Miss Nellie Jones came upon a strawberry of mammoth proportions, measuring five inches round; the paper fails to document its taste. In winter, icy strata were chiseled out of Crystal Lake, a foot thick and sometimes thicker, and in August 1909, a Reverend A. T. Everett, while fishing for pout, snared a five-pound eel stretching the length of his arm.

A Mr. Kitchen wrote impassioned editorials on the benefits of raising dairy cows, and another man, unnamed, wrote remonstrations to the town about the quantity of freely roaming cattle meandering along the hill roads of Gilmanton. Residents were a superstitious lot; they threw horseshoes to ward off witches and read the rise of wildcats and bears as omens of the town's moral degradation.

Men discovered Indian tomahawks buried in their fields, thieves went after chicken roosts, woodpiles and clotheslines, and a beekeeper in the 1880s arranged to be stung no less than thirty times consecutively in the hope of making himself immune to stings altogether. The paper reports the experiment a success.

To entertain, picnics, dinners and corn husking parties were held (one amassing a tower two hundred golden ears high). Women laid out suppers of chicken pie, gravy, green peas, sweet mixed pickles, cranberry sauce and pineapple ice cream; they traded recipes for squash pie. Once seventy-six men and women snuck out into the night carrying cakes and ice cream; the temperature registered 24 below, but this was hardly a deterrent for a planned surprise anniversary celebration. A plough match, comparing seven of the latest field models, drew crowds of two hundred; and one cold January afternoon, a bevy of young men abandoned their axes to go tearing down the hill to catch a glimpse of the crushing power of a new snow plough.

Time has transformed the ordinaries of life. Distinct voices animate the crinkled graying pages of town history:

> During the shower of June 28th, lightening struck and killed the most valuable cow in the herd of Nehemiah Durgin. What seems remarkable is that this was the only visible flash of lightning. (*News and Critic,* July 7, 1909)

> The conditions of rascality in these parts are fierce. Last Monday evening, October 21, two little scamps, George Albec and Carlton Smith, almost scared some of our good people to death with pumpkins, cut into horrible masks, and fearsomely illuminated with candles inside until they gleamed with a ghastly, ghoulish glow. Why are such things allowed? (*News and Critic,* November 9, 1921)

> Carl Jones is cutting the bushes between the road and Loon Pond, which makes a big improvement in the shore of the pond but the question arrives where will the boys go when they wish to change their clothing? Will they follow the example of the Camp Fire Girls and change at home? (*News and Critic,* February 3, 1926)

One Hundred and Sixty-Four Years

GILMANTON RESIDES IN THE LOWER wedge of Belknap County, one of ten towns. Two of those towns and the tip of a third once were included within Gilmanton lines. They have since split off, throwing their hands up in exasperation when snow and mud kept them from voicing opinions at town meetings. But before the towns broke away, before America fought against England and won, before the Abenaki tribes fought against the settlers and lost, Gilmanton was sketched in sticks and stones. On maps and in the land itself, Gilmanton's corners were weighted down with specific trees: beech, birch and hemlock.

In March of 1731, nine men set out into the woods. They carried with them chisels and hammers. Over the course of a fortnight, the nine carved the town's initials into the terrain. They:

> began at a Beech tree standing at the corner of Barnstead,
> Chichester, and Gilmanton, marked B.C.G.; and ran thence
> 6 miles North East to a White Birch, which they marked G.;

thence North West 2 miles to a Beech, also marked with the letter G.; thence North to Winepisockit Pond, 7 miles, to a Hemlock marked with a G.

From the pink armchair in his living room, David Bickford can visualize for me the route they would have taken, because he has walked the same lines more than two centuries later in fulfilling his official duties. In eighteen years as a town selectman, David has perambulated Gilmanton's silhouette on three occasions. "We went out on Saturdays, usually four or five Saturdays in a row." With a selectman from a bordering town, David has trod the town's profile, one angle a day. They carried compasses and previous selectmen's renditions of the boundaries:

Thence N81E about the east side of Walnut Mnt. About 160 rods to a large brown boulder in the Powell lot (formerly Russell pasture) about 20 rods East of a wood road and between two brooks. Marked 91-98-05-12-26-33-40-47-54-61.

The going, he recalls, was at times slow. The original trees into which the nine men carved the town's initials have long since come crashing down. Under state ordinance, they have been replaced with new markers by the town selectmen who walk the lines of Gilmanton—a task they must repeat every seven years for time eternal. Into the land, David and those who came before him have carved again and again their claim—into elm trees, oak trees, spruce, maple, beech, pine. Into yellow birch, hemlock and buckhorn. They have chiseled dates into four-foot boulders and onto piles of stone. Great numbers have been embedded into stone walls. Others have been tapped into stone posts protruding upwards out of moss. There are nearly seventy markers in all—placed on mountaintops and beside ponds, planted along roads and sunk into swamps. With time, markers are reclaimed by the land. New candidates are selected and engraved. Along the Alton line, a hemlock substitutes for a fallen beech. On a road bordering Belmont, a resilient stone post has replaced a lost birch. And on Route 129, formerly Hollow Road, leading toward Loudon, a misplaced stone has been superseded by a highway marker fashioned from cement.

> Thence on the same course to a stone in the Townline wall near the corner of the Michael Freil meadow about 70 feet from a wood road in a Northerly direction about 33 feet from the end of the wall, rock on the East side of the wall and at the base of wall. Above mentioned wood road follows south side of swamp and leaves main road about 100 feet South of the Steven Brook Bridge. Stone marked X-12-33-26-40-47-54-61-61 added 76.

Curious after visiting David, I walked out into the woods in search of border stones. On a hot August afternoon I walked up the same dirt road described by centuries-old selectmen. Now the road leads to a boy's camp. Walking along the left edge of the road I easily located the toothy remnants of a wall. With no camp boys in sight, I climbed half on to the wall, running my fingers over the stone. I felt cracks from age, jagged ribbons of mica, patches of pillowing moss and flaky lichen, but found no intentional fissures that formed unquestionable letters.

I am not the only one to get lost searching for border stones.

"One of the stones was in a dairy farm and the farmers kind of muddled things up for us in there," David muses. This particular border stone was of special importance as it was the meeting place of four towns.

"This stone, quite a big stone, sat on a rock pile and it had all the dates carved into it." Waving his hand, David sketches the stone. "Well, the farmers had been in there clearing that field. And they proceeded to roll that stone off and down a ways. The Barnstead selectman and I, we were both pretty rugged then. We were able to roll that thing back and get it on that pyramid of rocks and put it in the right position. You had to turn it so the markings would face the respective towns."

> Beginning at the Gilmanton–Gilford–Belmont corner, a flat stone on the ground, on the west side of the wall, about 215 feet south of the Durrell Mnt. Road. Marked 1863-70-77-84-91-05-12-33-40-47-54-61-G-B-X.

David continues to another story of stones, this one at the Gilmanton-Gilford-Belmont intersection. After carving their number into the flat face of the stone, David on whim decided to clamber up on to the wall and straddle it like a horse. Reaching one long arm up, over and down, he succeeded in tickling the grass on each side—playing Twister in three towns at once.

Again in search of stones, I drove out to find this tri-town corner. Durrell Mountain Road, the road referred to in the description of the town boundary, still exists, though it extends up into the woods unmaintained. I drove as far as I could and then continued on foot, hiking alone into the woods. Overconfident,

I hiked with my pens and my notepads and my camera, but no compass or GPS. After walking for what I figured to be a mile, I began detouring along each stone wall I found, following them a ways as they branched from the road. I found plenty of expansive flat stones, but no chiseled chronologies. I did find a black bear mud bathing. Startled by each other's abrupt appearance, we stared at one another. And then with a sigh, the bear galumphed off into the marsh. With my own sigh of relief I turned around and trekked quietly back out of the woods.

Long before David could straddle a stone wall and balance in three towns simultaneously, Gilmanton was larger. So large, that the stone wall in question lay entirely in Gilmanton. Back then, the town was puzzle-pieced into an array of villages: Meredith Bridge Village, Gilford Village, Lake Village, Factory Village, James Town, Tioga and Hurricane. There was included an upper Gilmanton (now part of Belmont), a lower Gilmanton, a Central Gilmanton (now the Corners) and an East Gilmanton (more central than east). East of East Gilmanton was Gilmanton Iron Works. At the turn of the twentieth century, a presumptuous visitor from Massachusetts sent around a petition to change its name to East Gilmanton. He believed it would read better on vacationers' postcards. The town disagreed. Iron Works it remained.

Selectman is a uniquely New England occupation. In Gilmanton, they come in threes. Most serve one three-year term, sometimes two. In a row, David served six. When David held office, he took charge of the town's assessments, walking the town's properties and recording them all in a blotter book

he kept by his armchair. Routinely David inked pages each night after work, keeping lights on past eleven o'clock, past midnight. On election days, David counted ballots starting at 7 a.m. and ending at 6 a.m. the following morning. A selectman's pay is honorific only. "I was curious once and one evening I decided to calculate my hourly wage." Laughing, David admits, "It came to 35 cents."

Exchanging his selectman's duties, David joined the town budget committee for three terms, moderator of the village district for a century's quarter. For the Pine Grove Cemetery, David devoted nine years as caretaker, acted as sexton for thirteen, managed finances for twenty-two, and shared directorial duties for forty.

Of his service, David says only "I don't begrudge the time I donated to the town. I felt that I was doing my civic duty." Added consecutively, David's years of service to the town are of Biblical proportions: 164 years in all.

> Thence on the same course to a post on the North side of the road by the land of John Warburton and near the Northwest corner of land formerly owned by Walter B. Page.

A stone, resembling an oversized upright tinker toy, is discernable at the junction of Beauty Hill and Hatch Road. So far it is the only marker I have successfully located in my own wanderings of the town's perimeter. The stone is visible in a peripheral sort of way, the eye noting its presence in the first blink and dismissing it by the second. The granite post thumbtacks a stone wall to the earth. It is here where Gilmanton ends.

I climbed into the brush, ducking under low hanging branches and skirting a patch of poison ivy. Crouching next to the stone I felt its ridges with my open palm. Facing west, a G proclaiming Gilmanton is carved large and rounded, its curves softened in the manner of museum statues after countless hands have rubbed away precision. When peered at it from an angle, the letter appears to dissipate into stone. Facing east, a B, for Barnstead, dominates the stone face, the writer's hand thin, deep, and spiked. Arrayed across the stone is a bingo board's worth of numbers. They are jumbled two-digit dates. They are carved out of order on the stone, mostly marking seven-year increments, though not always.

61: In a firm script right below the B. Also a 68 on the slanted stone crown and nestled between quartz veins. Both numbers carved by David.

40: Before World War II, the town's residents slipped away leaving barely seven hundred. Succession took over as pine trees reclaimed acres of abandoned land.

1887: H. H. Holmes, once a Mudgett and now a doctor, bigamist and killer, traveled cross-country. He met, wooed, and married a young woman of Minneapolis, who became the second of three wives he would attain.

05: A quiet year in the timeline of Gilmanton, the number in stone just as subtle. History records the closing of a two-room school, but hardly more.

47: On impulse Lizzie followed David deer hunting. She marked the occasion by shooting a buck, which they mounted on their wall, where to this day it stares unblinking. David bought Lizzie a .30-30 bolt action of her own and took her deer hunting from then on. David himself would shoot his last of thirty-two deer at the age of seventy-nine.

In the progression of seven-year etchings, I feel for a 26 that David has told me should be there—but I am unsuccessful. Somewhere too must be a 33. After three years of courtship, David proposed to Lizzie in 1933. They were married in the Iron Works' parsonage, a two-dollar wedding with David's sister as sole guest. Rings exchanged, the newlyweds drove off to the White Mountains for the weekend.

54: A town called Peyton Place was born.

19: This would be the year Gilmanton residents, perhaps in their fields or along the river, heard a drone and would bend their necks upwards to catch their first glimpse of a plane.

76: The script is small and the numbers coated in a layer of lichen. This is the last of three that David carved into this stone marker, standing just back from the woods at the border of Gilmanton and Barnstead.

On my next visit to David I ask him about the stone. As with so many things about the town, he smiles in recognition. "76" was the last date he carved into the granite, indeed into any of the seventy or so stones, posts, boulders and trees lacing the town. "We carved it on a Saturday in late November," he pauses. "The ground was firm because there had recently been a frost." He does not mention, but I calculate in my head that he would have been sixty-three at the time. The chiseling, he recalls, took no more than five minutes. "We had a narrow chisel like you would cut iron with and a hammer," David describes. "There was a knack to doing it. If you set the chisel on it and hit it, it wouldn't work right. But by having a loose grip on it and just tapping, you let it bounce into wherever you wanted it to go. Little by little your hand would slip down the chisel and you'd bring it back up again. And you would just keep tapping."

At Rest

GIVE DAVID BICKFORD almost any inhabitant of Gilmanton and he will list their profession, genealogy, directions to their homestead, cause of death and, in many cases, their burial site—not only the cemetery but directions to the gravestone. To find the resting place of Asa Edgerly, drive up the unmaintained Edgerly Road off of Stage Road and head to the upper corner of Hillside Cemetery. Asa, as David tells us, was the father of Carrie Leyland, who once lived in our house. Asa was also the grandfather to little Esther Edgerly, whose father died in an elevator accident up in Laconia when she was only twelve and who was raised by three elderly relatives. The grave of Esther's father, George, can also be found in the upper edge of Hillside Cemetery.

Before death by elevators, men and women were likely to suffer death from fire, water (many while in the process of bathing), and by plummeting tree limbs. Others choked on bones or beans. Lancaster, David's historical predecessor, records them all: the man who, while sleeping, walked out a third story window and the fellow who expired in a pasture, a jug of rum tucked like a teddy bear under his arm. A woman was felled by lightning in the process of haying during the Sabbath, and another struck suddenly dead in the midst of a religious revival. On January 19, 1807, almost forty-six years to the month of his arrival, Benjamin Mudgett, Gilmanton's first settler, opened his door to step out into the snow, perhaps to take a breath of fresh air, smacked his head on the lintel and collapsed dead.

In wandering Gilmanton I have grown surprisingly fond of graveyards. I take off on my bike with a notebook crammed in a pocket and wander through the mossy moguls of the deceased to track down characters I have read about in the basement museum or dusty tomes.

Smith Meeting House Cemetery caters to some of the most ancient Gilmanton inhabitants. Joseph Philbrick presides, age 288. Cracked and sheer, the original stone dozes on the shoulder of a stouter, more handsome marker bearing his name, his age at death (51) and the year he died (1776.) The inscription, which denotes him as the first to be buried in the cemetery, fails to detail the cause of death—a fall from the Meeting House roof, or his occupation—Gilmanton's first blacksmith. The cemetery is wrapped in wrought iron frills—an arch of silhouetted swirls.

There are at least thirty-nine burial sites throughout the town of Gilmanton. Most contain less than two dozen graves. Forgotten family graves tucked into forest glens, far back from the road. Edgerly Cemetery, with thirteen bearing the family name and one incongruous Hunkins. Two Sanborn burial sites bookend the town. Merrill cemetery has four graves, French eleven. There are Guinea Ridge, Range Road, Wilson Hill, Weed, Tibbetts, Carr, Sleeper, Osgood, Page, Plummer, Foss. Levi Hutchinson is all alone in the woods and wreathed in stone. Harry Besse is accounted for twice. His body lies with his second wife, Geraldine North, in Besse Cemetery; another stone bearing his name stands sheepishly beside his first wife, Olive Besse, in Smith Meeting House Cemetery. Emerson Cemetery displays only two stones, but the earth dips and swells, suggesting unmarked brethren. In modern graveyards, grassy mounds indicate the location of the dead; here, the opposite is usually true. It is the dips that count—wooden coffins having long rotted and collapsed inwards. Stones have fared only moderately better. In the smaller cemeteries, they protrude like aged teeth, chipped or worn down with time to mossy gums. Inscriptions are scarce. Weather and mottled lichen have erased names and days and years. While David was once a sexton of the town, it is Marion McIntyre, a Gilmanton Cemetery trustee, I seek out for her fastidious documentation of the town's dead.

At Smith Meeting House Cemetery, the headstones stand stately. Those that have hunched with age or succumbed to cracks have been smoothly repaired. Cement veins run crooked in the stone. The lawns are mowed, and no saplings shoot up between the graves. Only aged, scaly-skinned sugar maples umbrella the stones. The Cemetery is one of four still in use (the others are Pine Grove, Beech Grove and Buzzell) and the variety of stones is testament to over two centuries of death: thin flakes of stone, rough edged; thick slabs of creamy marble, black marble; and large-nosed cherubs, spread winged, stare wide-eyed.

Stone willow branches sag. A carved lamb crowns the grave of a twelve-year-old Julia Ann. Some dead prefer fieldstones, massive irregular hulks of granite dragged from the pastures. Near the road, Mr. James Ham has carried a sense of humor to the grave. His selected boulder, coppery and cone-shaped, was chosen to resemble a giant's pork feast.

In many of the cemeteries, stones no longer mark the dead. Until 1986, it was legal for old tombstones to be sold and carried away. Only a solitary stone remains in Sawyer Lake Cemetery, propped against a tree. Marion McIntyre suspects the large hole in Lydia Leavitt's stone spared it from theft. In 1992, eleven markers were returned to Copp Cemetery. Sturbridge Village, a tourist attraction in central Massachusetts, recreating a nineteenth-century village, had purchased them for twenty-five dollars a head; they believed the stones added authenticity to their ersatz graveyard.

The dead lie everywhere in Gilmanton. Cemeteries are not all confining. A Stanley Wicka is buried in a family's lawn, a Ruth Jones in a basement. Lumps behind a barn mark the site of four graves, with only one name recorded: Mrs. D. In the woods, a woman and her four children succumbed to spotted fever; they rest under a grove of pines.

I have been told that a former slave is shuffled into the deck of stones that make up Smith Meeting House Cemetery. David cannot confirm, so late in the summer, I went searching, but without success. I found instead the raised brick tomb of Gilmanton's first minister, Isaac Smith, his history worked into slate. His age: 72. The college he attended: "Princeton College." On the roll of the hill, where the cemetery droops down toward the trees, huddles the most ancient collection of stones—like doting elders. The tombstones claim dates of death that predate Mr. Philbrick by as much as two years, but no plaque proclaims them as most aged. At the top of Frisky Hill more than a mile off, bodies long dissolved into dust sleep under blankets of asphalt. Only their stones have made the trek to Smith Meeting House when their own cemetery was paved over. The infamous Grace Metalious lies ostracized in a far corner butting up against pines. Her grave is white and unadorned, just her name and the dates of her life: 1924-1964. It is this particular lump, Alice Bean says, that still feels the pound of dancing feet on the night of February 25, the anniversary of the author's death. Someone has planted pompom mums and long stemmed lilies up close to the stone.

There are four burial sites along Stage Road, two flanking our house, less than a mile apart. Hillside Cemetery lies bald and blotchy within the woods. Near the edge, where maple leaves have receded from the stone wall, are the graves of previous inhabitants of our house—Edgerlys, Fellows, Spanglers—members of the family who constructed the homestead over two hundred years ago. Pine Grove Cemetery is larger, with 939 dead, flat and expansive in an open field. Small lanterns set by particular graves, along with pansies and flags, at night become glowing eyes—orange, green and eerie in the consuming dark. A lopsided sign fastened to the gate commands: "No horses or ATVs allowed."

I have ridden horses in Beech Grove Cemetery close to the Corners. The cemetery is less conventional, knobbly with pockets of grave-filled glens sequestered in the woods, ideal for trail riding. Levi Mudgett, the father of the mass murderer H. H. Holmes, is buried here, though his son is not. Holmes, formerly Herman Webster Mudgett, was interred face down in cement ten feet under in a Pennsylvania graveyard after his execution. When I returned on foot to Beech Grove, I came in search of one particular stone. I perused every marker before successfully finding it. Moses N. Dustin, a private in the Massachusetts 54th, the first all-black regiment of the Civil War, celebrated in the movie *Glory*. A New Hampshire farmer, Dustin survived the doomed charge on Fort Wagner in South Carolina. He settled in Gilmanton and lived to the age of sixty-five, dying before the century's turn. His white marble grave stands resolute, back turned to the crowd of others.

Returning to Smith Meeting House Cemetery, I discover that it was Thomas Cogswell who owned the former slave: an Alice H. Cogswell, whose stone stands in the middle of the cemetery. Her grave is small, marbled white, elaborately crowned—her age: sixteen; her year of death: 1876. An inscription reads: "Granddaughter of Prince." Records do not indicate whether the "Prince" was a name or a title. George Roberts Jr., recounts how the Cogswells brought slaves from the South, freeing them in the North. "They were Congregationalists. They didn't believe in slavery. They shared a church pew with them."

The cemeteries of Gilmanton are seasoned with many of the same names. Families that arrived in centuries past have had children, grandchildren and great-grandchildren. In a town of less than four thousand, few of the names have died with their original bearers: Cogswell, Clough, Coffin, Hussey, Ross, Eastman, Thing, Burgess, Badger, Geddes, Kitchen, Lougee, Price, Potter, Edgerly, Gilman.

Only 104 gravestones bear the surname Gilman. Undoubtedly there are more gravesites, buried into the hillsides and valleys of Gilmanton. But only 104 stones remain intact. In a town where once every third resident bore the name Gilman, the lineage has dwindled to less than one in three thousand. Exactly one Gilman now lives in Gilmanton—Paula Gilman, who traces her ancestry back, back, back to Edward Gilman Jr. one of twenty-four Gilmans granted land in New Hampshire.

Today, other names populate the town. Bean, Barns, Morse, Jarvis, Geddes, Bickford, Lander. But the name adopted by the town two centuries ago remains.

—m—

Lizzie Bickford rests within the cemeteries of Gilmanton. She died when I was seventeen and she was ninety-six. She outstripped Hannah Mudgett, Gilmanton's first woman settler, by a year—nearly two centuries of history added between them. She died at the start of June and was buried in the open lawn of Pine Grove Cemetery. "No horses or ATVs allowed." I was abroad at the time, studying in South America, and could not attend the funeral. But when I returned to Gilmanton later that summer I went searching in the cemetery. The grave stone is long, squat and slanted back—gray marble with a rugged edge. Lizzie's name is carved to the left. David's name is already carved beside hers, keeping her company.

Within two years of Lizzie's death, David sold their small white cape with the forest green shutters, and quietly left Gilmanton. He moved to Gilford, two towns to the north and purchased a much smaller house near that of his daughter. He had lived in the same house on Stage Road for seventy years minus two months.

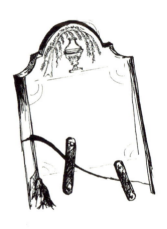

They Speak for Themselves

ONE HUNDRED AND EIGHTY POUNDS of beans—pea and kidney—need to be lowered into the ground. To accomplish the feat, the Gilmanton Fire Department has been radioed in. There are six in all, nearly one fourth of the force, including the chief but not including the Belknap County Sheriff, who stands stiffly to the side, gun holster hanging conspicuously from his waist. Four five-foot pits are lined with stones and ringed with firemen and other muscled volunteers who stand idle for now, watching as the last of the beans are seasoned. Above, there is a salting of clouds, the August air warm; it is 6:30 p.m. the night before Gilmanton's 111th annual Old Home Day celebration.

To raise town funds in 1891, a fair was held on the lawn skirting Smith Meeting House. Tables were laid with lace, a gramophone was sent whirling, and two hundred townspeople convened for supper. The event was such a success that it was repeated the following summer, and again the summer after that.

At the turn of the century, future governor Frank Rollins,

concerned that the townspeople of New Hampshire were slipping southward, sent out a call.

Sons and daughters of New Hampshire, wherever you are, listen to the call of the old Granite State! Come back, come back!…Is there any spot more sacred to you than the place where you were born? No matter how far you have wandered, no matter how prosperous you have been, no matter what luxurious surroundings you now have, there is no place quite like the place of your nativity… . I wish that in the ear of every son and daughter of New Hampshire, in the summer days, might be heard whispered the persuasive words: Come back, come back! "New Hampshire's Opportunity." (*The New England Magazine*. Volume 22, Issue 5, July 1897.)

And the people came. As the air began to turn crisp in the August haze, tables and tents were erected in towns across the state. In 1902, the Gilmanton fair was renamed and the first annual Old Home Day was held.

—ᴍ—

For an hour now, the beans have been simmering on the stove, a big black gas burner heating a corner of the Cook House, which has stood in some form on or near this spot for more than a century. In the Cook House, Ginny Hiltz presides. She has commanded the cooking of the beans for going on twenty-eight years. "My mother-in-law warned me that one of the family commitments was Old Home Day!" Ginny is small at under five feet six; her personality is not. For reading recipes, she dons

thin-rimmed glasses whose stems burrow into cropped and peppered curls. Today, she dresses in shorts and a blue T-shirt, a crock of beans emblazoned across the midriff: "Gilmanton Old Home Day Beanhole Beans. They Speak For Themselves."

—⁂—

Before there was a meetinghouse, the parsons of Gilmanton addressed their followers in parlors, schoolrooms, and horse barns. The first town-employed minister, Isaac Smith, up from Connecticut, preached his sermons as a nomad for sixteen years. As the historian Daniel Lancaster details, Smith was "tall and slender in his person, [and] rather bony." In the winter, when furnaces were scorned as indulgences, Smith's broad shoulders were made larger still by overcoats. With frost transforming windowpanes into monochromatic stained glass, Smith often orated in mittens.

In 1774, the skeleton of a meetinghouse, sixty feet by forty-five feet, and bookended by open-air porches, was raised skywards. A year later came a roof, then a floor, a pulpit and pews. Funds were as sparse as residents, and construction was heavy with intermissions. Funds would be found, though, in 1778, when the town sold for 180 pounds Lot 18, situated on the banks of Crystal Lake, then Lougee Pond, to a Mr. Moses Morrill who dreamed of creating an iron works. Smith's meetinghouse sat incomplete for twelve additional years, a service paused before the communal amen. The final trimmings and curtains were financed not with coin, but with donated hundred-pound portions of beef and bushels of corn, which were used as reimbursement for the supplies and worker's pay. Payment in beans is not mentioned, though not improbable.

In Pelham, New Hampshire, on Old Home Day, residents grill BBQ chicken and boil corn on the cob. They serve the same in Hollis and Weare. There are hot dogs and pizza in Campton, and in Londonberry they ply returnees with pancakes. In Gilmanton, we bake beans. Originally the women of Gilmanton would each prepare their own beans according to trusted family recipes. However, the practice bred favorites and, in equal portion, resentment by cooks whose beans went unconsumed. In the 1960s, a father-and-son team dug the first communal fire pits and lined them with stones pulled from the surrounding field. When more beans and consequently more pits were required, backhoes were summoned. To fit into the pits, the town borrowed pots of kettle-drum proportions from one Shirley Marden. The town is still borrowing them today.

Into each of the four cauldron-sized cast-iron pots Ginny oversees the layering of ingredients: a generous helping of beans, a thin drizzle of molasses, a line of brown sugar, a dusting of spices, slabs of salt pork, another helping of beans and so on. Edible strata accumulate in the cauldrons. Years earlier, when Ginny first marched into the Cook House, her predecessor, Sybil Bryant, instructed her to mix the seasonings by hand. Ginny complied, one arm gloved past the elbow in molasses, only to find Sybil laughing uproariously. Filled, each pot will have consumed one gallon of molasses, four pounds of brown sugar, over ten pounds of salt pork, water up to the rim, an undisclosed quantity of spices and beans—fifty pounds of pea or forty pounds of kidney. When latched and screwed tight, the pots resemble overturned land tortoises in both size and weight.

The beans are ready to lower. Chains are wrapped around a long, polished beam and the firemen take up their stance. The beam is of horn wood, a member of the birch family with a notably smooth surface. For the fires, dry maple and ash is preferred. "These beans are hard work! Who'd have thought!" grunts one of the men. Even a slight tip sends muddy bean water dribbling down the pot sides. In a quiet moment, I inquire of one of the firemen if this is the oddest call the fire department has received. It's not, he says, but doesn't elaborate. The fire chief, who has been on the job less than three weeks, is taking the task in stride. He paces back and forth behind the pit, leaning over to inspect his men's handiwork.

—⁓—

Accompanying the bean-hole dinner, there is always a fair, similar in many ways to the one that materializes on the Academy lawn for the Fourth of July—only larger. Stands sell watercolors, antique clothing, birdhouses perched on rakes, shovels, and pitchforks. The Gilmanton Women's Club has decorated a table; so too have the Lower Gilmanton Community Club, the Gilmanton Historical Society, and the Year Round Library Organization. Summers back, I set up a stand—using ladders as shelves to display homemade soaps and painted wooden bookshelves carved like animals.

The Meeting House is not alone on the lawn. When driving up Meeting House Road, the first thing that appears out of the foliage is the steep embankment of the Smith Meeting House cemetery. Between it and the Meeting House stands another building, smaller but of similar construction—the former Smith Meeting House School. Gilmanton's original 1727 charter necessitated the construction of schools, although it mentioned no precise count. By the early eighteen hundreds, twenty single- or double-room schoolhouses were in session, including Rogers School, Sanders School and Sanborn School. There was of course the school in the Iron Works, attended by David Bickford, and an opposing one in the Corners. There were Lamprey, Lougeetown, Jones' Mill, Allen's Mill, Gale, Griffin and Guinea Ridge. And Kelley School in Lower Gilmanton, built in 1778 and still maintained, just back from the road. And there was Potter School, now a house, just west of Geddes farm.

Mary Morse attended the one-room Potter School in the Roaring Twenties with ten other kids—depending on the season. Her brother, Duncan (the namesake of the present day, blueberry-raking Duncan Geddes), was the sole boy in the school. The Potter School had a harmonica band, the Kelley School a rhythm band. If the Smith Meeting House School's pupils expressed musical talent, it has gone unrecorded. Mary doesn't play the harmonica anymore. "Do you know what happens?" she says, laughing. "My false teeth come out!"

As a young woman, Lizzie Bickford baked and cooked pies, casseroles and beans at the Iron Works school—the same two-roomer David attended as a boy. Blueberry pies, peach pies and apple pies, like the kind she used to bake us. Chuck Price had a particular fondness for her soups. "Fridays were my favorite cause she made corn chowder," he pauses, tasting fifty-year-old meals in his mind. "She tried pea soup once, but I don't think hardly a kid ate it." Kids in David's time did not enter the classroom until age eight. David walked into first grade of the Iron Works School after Mud Vacation, known in cities as March Break. School recessed in June and on his return in September, David moved right along into second grade. For good measure he finished third grade in the same term. Grades four through eight he explored at a more sedate pace, limiting himself to one a year. With the nearest high school seven miles down a dirt road, David capped his formal education on graduating eighth grade with a class size of two. Managing the town taxes as a selectman years later, David worried that some might balk at his lack of proper schooling. No one ever did.

In the Cook House, things are heating up. Yesterday evening's brown breads, armored in aluminum, are now stacked in the oven—forty-eight bread bricks in all. Pages of pink ham and pats of butter are plated and are stacked in the fridge. Competing for space are buckets of coleslaw; forty-five pounds of cabbage shiny with Ginny's secret dressing: "You can't have it even if you torture me." With condiments and sides prepared and the beans still hibernating underground, all that is left to do is to slice and plate pies.

Last night, ovens all across Gilmanton were set to 400 degrees; pies served on Old Home Day are baked by town residents and are just as diverse. We slice into pecan pies, strawberry rhubarb pies and apple pies filled with Gilmanton apples. Townswomen have rolled their pies thick, and they have rolled them thin and flaky. Certain crusts are as pale as a birch bark, while others resemble flecked spruce. Then there are lattice-faced peach pies, open-faced pumpkin pies and peaked meringues. Sixty-two tins. Twenty π in all. Blueberry Cream Cheese, Chocolate Cream, Chocolate Meringue, Cherry, Brownie. Blueberry pies are abundant and temperamental: some slice clean and others are hardly more than soup in a tin.

Old Home Day, which runs from midmorning to midafternoon, is woven with activities. In years past, there have been musket firing, tomahawk throwing and horseshoe tossing. Most years, antique cars are revved up to chug through the yard; one year, Victorian fashion was shaken out and donned for procession. Some years, there are plays. A century ago, Mary Morse's parents first met as actors in one such performance, after a young boy never showed for rehearsal and a scrawny Geddes' boy took his place alongside Mary's mom. This year, in addition to the cars, Cheryl Barnes has brought two of her Tiny Tails horses and Larry Frates has brought his magic tricks. Alice and Stan Bean are wandering amongst the booths. So too is Barbara Geddes—blueberry season is waning. "Only three more days I reckon. They are shriveling up like raisins."

David Bickford has returned to Gilmanton. Weeks ago on a visit to his house in Gilford we had attempted to convince him to

attend Old Home Day. At the time he had vacillated. If he were
to attend, he explained, a cane would be a necessary companion
to map out the uneven turf. And as he reminds us, a cane would
make him look "like an old geezer!" But, on this occasion David
has forgone concerns about appearing decrepit. He walks slowly,
but determined, and the metal tipped cane he employs appears
stately rather than required. Kids dart in and out of the crowd
on scavenger hunts that send them into the sprawling cemetery
beside the schoolhouse and down into the art show held in the
basement of the Meeting House.

—∭—

Twenty-five disgruntled men and women abandoned Smith
Meeting House to build their own church in the years leading
up to the Civil War, the Centre Congregational Church that sits
kitty-corner to the Academy in the Corners. Fifteen more left
soon after, perhaps in retaliation, to form their own congregation in the Iron Works. Already Gilmanton hosted a Free Will
Baptist Church, a religious response to the raising of Smith
Meeting House, constructed in the same year. A replica built
in the mid-eighteen hundreds still stands steepled in Lower
Gilmanton. For a time there would be another Free Will Baptist
Church in the Iron Works, but it would burn like brimstone in
1915. In varying decades of town history, Gilmanton would hear
sermons by Methodists and sermons by the Society of Friends.
In the modern day, the town is addressed by Congregationalists
and Assemblies of God. Recent reconciliation has led the church-
es in the Iron Works and the Corners to unite. The congregation

Ping-Pongs weekly between the two locations.

Reverend Isaac Smith orated for forty-three years in the town of Gilmanton, mittens and all; when he died, he was buried only yards from his pulpit in the adjoining cemetery. Smith was succeeded by a Reverend Spofford, who was followed by none other than the historian Daniel Lancaster himself. Lancaster does not record his own short tenure, but soon after, the Meeting House, which had aged poorly, was pulled to the ground. In its place, and from the same wood, a smaller church was erected. This new church was no longer a meetinghouse, nor was it presided over by Minister Smith; however, Smith Meeting House it remained.

—⋙—

The firemen have returned, busy shoveling sand off of the bean pits. Overnight the beans rested under blankets of plastic tarp and piles of sand. Steam billows in the process of uncovering, and the pots are hoisted ever so slowly out and onto the grass. Folks gather as the lids are unscrewed and slid off to reveal umber liquid with the vague outline of beans below. Ginny is in the middle, glasses clouded with steam. She dips a spoon. The crowd is silent, all eyes on Ginny. She does not disappoint, smacking her lips in satisfaction. "These are as good as they ever were!"

With the beans bowled and sent out to the diners, Ginny wanders amongst the tables. Sometimes she stops and chats, but she doesn't sit and she doesn't take a serving of beans. Ginny will eat her beans tomorrow, reheated or perhaps cold. She will freeze some for the fall. Does she cook much at home, I ask. "Who, me?" Ginny laughs. "Me? No, I hate cooking."

Elsewhere

WHEN WE VISIT David Bickford's home, we bring homemade peach jam. Strawberry and raspberry he declines; the seeds get lodged in his teeth. He makes us baloney sandwiches and serves home-baked lemon meringue pie. He laughs at how tall my brothers and I have grown. "So, Jessica, you're turning twenty-six this year...and that will be on November 30th." David enjoys rattling off my brothers' ages and birthdays. He grins at our looks of amazement. He assures my mom that he knows her age as well, but nods conspiratorially with her, "I learned long ago that women don't like to be reminded of their age."

When David moved from Gilmanton after Lizzie's death, he sold or gave away most of his possessions. But the living room remained intact. And with it came all of David's stories, his accounts and his memories.

There are the two pink armchairs, the floral print couch, the mottled brown rug. The police scanner no longer hums. Instead the TV is set to the Red Sox. David is diligent in recording the score, inning by inning, for every game. But mostly he tells stories that took place in Gilmanton.

He tells stories of the crow he trained to ride on his shoulder while biking down an unpaved Stage Road. He tells stories of storms and of dry spells—he can recall the number of inches that fell and how the tomato plants fared. He tells stories of growing up farming: weeding gardens for the elderly (fifteen cents an hour) and cutting cordwood ($1.75 an hour). He tells stories of feeding the cider press ($1.50 an hour) at Oscar Giles' farm—the remnants of the mill in the river on our land. "Oh gosh, we ran through fifty-five gallon barrels a day!" Families, he explains, would bring their own barrels to be filled with sweet cider, which would in time ferment to hard cider, and finally to vinegar. The McIntosh apples, he recalls, were particularly juicy. If I refrain from looking out the windows, it is not hard to imagine we are in Gilmanton.

—⁂—

New Hampshire is latticed into ten counties and nailed together with thirteen cities, twenty-two unincorporated places and two hundred and twenty-one towns. There are the towns of Dalton, Dixville, Dunbarton, Sunapee, Seabrook, Colebrook, Keene. There is a Littleton with over six thousand residents and a Stark, which is anything but, containing the eastern crags of the White Mountains and named after the revolutionary general John Stark, originator of the state motto "Live free or die."

Fittingly, there is a town called Freedom, and another christened Unity. There is Bridgewater and Waterville Valley. A

Sugar Hill, Sandwich, Orange and Rye. There is a Bethlehem, a Greenland, a Milan, a Lisbon, a Lebanon, a Dublin and a Troy, all within two hundred miles of each other. There are towns titled Lempster, Swanzey, Goshen, Acworth, Chichester, Errol, Epping.

Gilmanton is just one town out of two hundred and twenty-one in New Hampshire. David is just one man with a hundred years of well-dusted memories. Elsewhere, in other towns across New Hampshire, there are more stories to listen to, more memories to collect. They can be found in the shade of pine groves, along the sunny outcroppings of granite knolls and in the afternoon light of a living room. There are more farms to explore, tucked at the ends of more long dirt driveways. All one needs to do is walk slowly and listen, and occasionally step off the path and follow the remains of a meandering stone wall.

—⁂—

In Gilmanton, fewer and fewer people remember David Bickford. Those residents who do remember tend to be an older crowd, and they too are slowly trickling out of the town, to assisted living and to relatives in more populated pockets of New Hampshire. In Gilmanton, there are new faces, new families. But, at the Town Hall in Gilmanton Four Corners, there hangs a small, grayed photograph of three men and one woman standing around one of their town's selectmen, who is seated at the wide table with a pen in hand. David's face is intent as he applies his signature to the page—a contract with a neighboring town to ensure the continual policing of Gilmanton. David appears dapper in a dark blazer and a striped tie; his thinning hair is brushed back. He wears large, thin-rimmed glasses.

David relinquished his role as selectman thirty years ago, but he continues to closely watch his town. When a towering pine was uprooted by Hurricane Irene in 2011 and fell sideways onto the chimney of his old home, he knew within the day. David routinely informs us of happenings in Gilmanton before we, still residents of the town, become aware. It has been decades since David acted as a caretaker to our house in the Iron Works, but that doesn't prevent him from still keeping an eye out. "I was driving by the other day and saw that you had left the garage doors unlocked. I could tell by the way the knobs were turned. You should really lock the doors."

When we visit, we stay for hours. When we finally leave, the leaving is a drawn out affair. Each footfall is sounded in stories, one for each slow step as we pass through the living room, through the kitchen and to the door. David always walks us to the front door, where, on a side table, are neatly stacked newspapers gone limp from thorough reading. The mounted adolescent buck's head stares, a glassy-eyed sentinel in the foyer. It is the buck that Lizzie shot over sixty years ago when she and David went walking through the woods of Gilmanton.

When we reach the foyer, there are rounds of hugs. David holds the front door open and proceeds after us. From the porch, David watches as we climb into our car. He waves and he watches. Only when we have begun driving backwards out of the driveway, only then, does David slowly turn and head back inside.

September

By the time Labor Day is upon us there is no denying the end of summer. The air is thick with the smells of blackberries and crushed pine needles. We spend the last week collecting provisions from our favorite farms: eggs from Tiny Tails, chèvre from Heart Song Farm, pints of maple syrup from the Price Farm. Wild blueberry season has already past, but we've frozen berries in anticipation of winter. We amass bottles of locally brewed Meetinghouse Soda—peach, rhubarb, blueberry, cider and maple cream.

When we drive down to Massachusetts we turn left following the split rail fence down Stage Road. We pass the houses of family friends; we pass the turnoff to the Price Farm, then the turn off to the Geddes Farm, and then the Potter Farm. We pass a young cemetery and an old cemetery. Mostly we pass by forests, occasionally fields. On a flat stretch along the former Hollow Road the sandy shoulders are tangled with poison ivy and weeds. It is somewhere along this stretch that we pass by the cement highway marker that separates Gilmanton from the town of Loudon. The demarcation is indistinguishable amongst the brush.

—w—

I know Gilmanton in the fall, in the winter, and in the spring, but only framed in weekends. The town is quieter. As the end of August arrives, the summer families, those skirting Crystal Lake, lock up their beach houses, which are not insulated against New England winters, and drive to the city. We too drive to the city, but often, we return.

We return in the fall when the forests are a blazing inferno of scarlet, ochre, tawny. From our pumpkin patch we harvest squash. There are apples to pick, though not from the orchard on our land that David Bickford used to tend—the trees there have long since gone feral. Instead we frequent local orchards and pick bushels upon bushels of apples. Though Oscar Giles' cider mill is reduced to parallel logs in the riverbed, we turn a hand press to squeeze gallons that last for months.

We return in the winter. Only the pines and hemlocks and spruce retain their foliage. The ground is frozen with ice crystals and layered in snow. We build igloos, snow Jacuzzis, frosty libraries. We walk in the woods to find half-moon prints of white-tailed deer, the pad marks of coyotes and, sometimes, the signs of bear and moose. We take our sleds and aim them at the river, carving slicked shoots over repeated runs. The Suncook does not freeze. In our sleds, we bail just short of the river.

We return in the spring. Mud season. We tap a lone sugar maple out near the road, boil down the sap until only a pint of amber syrup remains and, if we are not watchful, that too vanishes in vapor. For the rest of our supply we drive the half-mile to Price Farm and come away with half-gallon jugs. At home, we boil and toss dark maple syrup in an arc across the snow, so that it hardens into taffy.

As a last hurrah to summer, the Gilmanton Fire Department holds a Labor Day party on the edge of Crystal Lake. It is a fundraiser, like those for which Lizzie Bickford once baked pies. There is none of the old fashioned at the lake. No antique cars, historical society booths, men driving oxen. The Labor Day party is held at night under neon lights, strung up and hazy with bugs. There are dart games, can tosses, revolving rope ladder competitions. Beer, hot dogs and loud stereo music that echoes off the surface of the lake.

Always there are fireworks. We park our car along the road near the southern tip of Crystal Lake. Here the water bottlenecks. The current picks up in the jostling transition from lake to river. Only a bend or two down are the mill remains and somewhere the remnants of an iron works. For the best view I clamber up the side of the car and sit on the roof. For a time the exuberance of the fireworks obscures the constellations. The night is raucous and smoky. When I was little I used to cover my ears. I don't anymore. I watch the explosions, and I watch their reflection. The lake is inky, subtle shades deeper than the ebony of the surrounding trees. As the fireworks' roar dissipates, I am left again with the quieter, ceaseless tumble of water over rocks, as the Suncook passes under the bridge, and onward into the forest.

In Memoriam

David Bickford has returned to Gilmanton. On March 17th 2013, thirty-two days shy of his one hundredth birthday, David passed away peacefully in his sleep. He was buried along Stage Road—the same road where he was born a century back. It is the same stretch of road where he was married, where he raised his daughter, and where he lived for nearly seventy years with his wife Lizzie. It is the same road along which I met David so many years ago when I first began listening to his stories. He lies now with his wife, side by side, shaded from the morning sun by towering pines and a few branching maples.

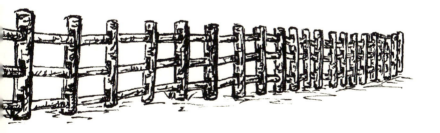

Acknowledgements

THE STORIES COLLECTED HERE are a testament to the generosity of the men and women of Gilmanton. Throughout my wanderings in the town, I have been fortunate to have remarkable teachers: Duncan, who taught me how to rake berries; Chuck, who showed me how to milk cows; Valerie, who instructed me in the art and science of cheese making; and Jim and Cheryl, who tutored me in the art of peach pruning, chicken tending, and miniature horse midwifery. To them and their entire families, I am deeply grateful.

The history of Gilmanton came alive for me through the vivid memories and careful research of many men and women who graciously shared their personal stories and their research. I particularly want to acknowledge Barbara Angevine, Lori Baldwin, Alice Bean, Lizzie Bickford, Sunny and Marshall Bishop, George and Sandy Burbank, Pat Clarke, John Dickey, Paula Gilman, Ginny Hiltz, Barbara McDermott, Sheila McDermott, Marion McIntyre, Mary Morse, George Roberts, Don and Donna

Rondolet, Esther Scammell, and Tom and Nancy Scribner.

I am grateful to the entire staff of Gilmanton's Town Hall, who graciously fielded my many questions and aided in my searches. I also relied on the memoirs of an older generation of residents who wrote careful and colorful histories that helped to animate the past.

Gilmanton has been part of my life for nearly two decades. As such, there are many more people who have been integral in helping me paint a picture of the town. To all those who I have not singled out by name, I want to offer my thanks.

The stories in this book were gathered over five years and capture particular moments in time. Life in Gilmanton has continued to change with the seasons—Jim Barnes' songwriting has blossomed into a career; the Year-Round Library has opened its doors; and the Gilmanton Museum has migrated to the Iron Works, becoming the newest tenant of Odd Fellows Hall.

This is my first book, and I have benefited from the wisdom of many. I want to thank Ellen Clegg, Elizabeth Gilmore, Marian Schlesinger, Andy Schlesinger and Bina Venkataraman for their advice and ideas. I am grateful to Janice Pieroni for helping me to navigate the publishing world. To the wonderful women in my extended family who read drafts and provided ideas, specifically Brooks Coe, Susan Frieden, Gish Jen, Ilana Manolson, Laurel Molk, Adrienne Raphel, Katie Walsh and Maryanne Wolf: thank you.

I have been blessed to have three creative and compassionate editors at Tide Pool Press. My deep thanks to Frank Herron for his rigorous attention to detail, to Ingrid Mach for her elegant design sensibility, and to Jock Herron for his generosity of spirit and his vision.

I owe much to two teachers for cultivating my passion for creative non-fiction. In high school, Sandy Stott gave us all notebooks and pencils and sent us to wander through our school and town, to listen closely and to write everything down. In college, I was fortunate enough to continue my exploration of the art of writing with Professor John McPhee as my guide. From John, I learned how to map the structure of a piece of writing, to strive to make every observation fresh and to polish paragraphs with lapidary care. By sharing your love and your mastery of the craft, you have both helped me to tell stories and thereby enriched my life.

To my brothers Daniel and David, who are my partners in exploration; to my mom Lori, who is my confidant and who shared with me her passion for capturing the world in art; to my dad Eric, who is my editor, my sounding board and who shares with me a passion for words: I love you all madly.

This book took form from the memories that David Bickford shared with me over twenty years. David passed away last spring before I could share with him what he had inspired me to write. I believe he would have approved. Most likely, he would have pulled out a red pen and, in his precise penmanship, added extra details amongst the lines of text. Last summer, I biked down to Pine Grove Cemetery and, digging a small hole next to his stone, planted a sprig of indigo forget-me-nots.

JESSICA LANDER is an avid explorer and a lover of stories. She has lived and taught in countries as far away as Thailand and Cambodia and in places as close as Massachusetts and New Jersey—teaching students from sixth grade to university. In addition to her freelance journalism, she writes an education-focused blog, *Chalk Dust*, about experiences in and out of the classroom. Growing up, Jessica spent her summers in Gilmanton, New Hampshire. She currently lives in her hometown of Cambridge, Massachusetts, near to family and friends.

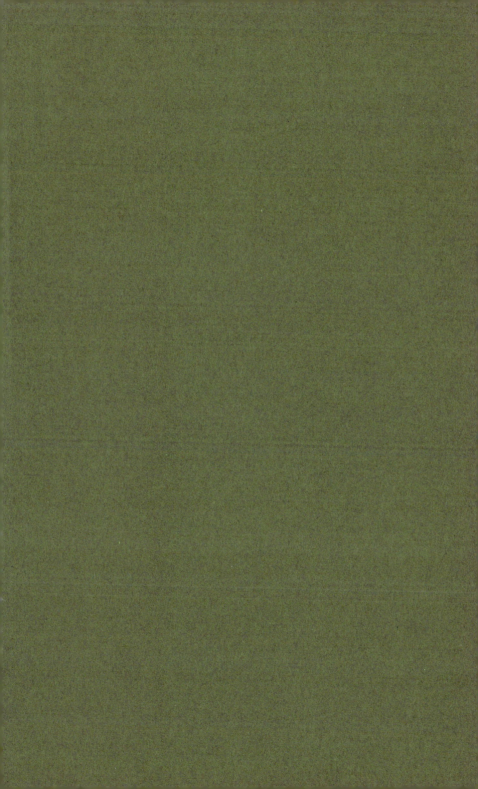